CONTENTS

Ships in Focus Publications

Correspondence and editorial:
Roy Fenton
18 Durrington Avenue,
London SW20 8NT
020 8879 3527
rfenton@rfenton.demon.co.uk

Orders and photographic:
John & Marion Clarkson
18 Franklands, Longton,
Preston PR4 5PD
01772 612855
sales@shipsinfocus.co.uk

Printed by Amadeus Press Ltd.,
Cleckheaton, Yorkshire.
Designed by Hugh Smallwood, John
Clarkson and Roy Fenton.

SHIPS IN FOCUS RECORD
ISBN 1 901703 74 6

SHIPS IN FOCU

July

CW00664102

Alex Duncan, well known amongst enthusiasts ...
negative collection and monthly photographic offers, died of a heart
attack in September 2003. As well as regret at his passing, there has
been much interest in Alex and the fate of his collection.

Alex was a very private person, but it is known that he was
an orphan, brought up by an aunt or great aunt. He lived for many
years near the Thames in Gravesend, moving to the Isle of Wight in
2001, a move which substantially lifted his spirits. Alex was
extremely generous in allowing his photographs to be used in a wide
variety of publications including *Record*, asking only for an
acknowledgement. Indeed, he wrote to us with a selection of his
photographs of Finnish ships which appeared in issue 26.

Alex first started advertising photos for sale about 1959,
beginning with a catalogue of some 8,000 titles taken post-war and
within a few months started photo offers in magazines, including
Marine News, which continued almost uninterruptedly until his
death. He offered prints from his own negatives taken on the
Thames and at Rotterdam and Hamburg, supplemented with
negatives acquired by exchanges with other photographers, and with
many others taken by the late Moffat Scott at Cape Town.

Alex left a collection of books to the World Ship Society and
in his will asked the Society to sell his negatives. Many people,
including Ships in Focus, hoped that the Society itself would acquire
the negatives and therefore the copyright. However, this was not to
be and his collection was bought by a private collector. This
collector was mainly interested in the non-British ships, so Ships in
Focus came to an arrangement with him to acquire the negatives of
British ships plus the small number of glass-plate negatives. This
was done in order to use them in *Record* and our other publications,
and we have agreed with the collector that we can include the non-
British ships when needed. We regret that at present we cannot see
a way to make offers of prints from the collection: our time and
energies are fully devoted to our publishing activities. Nevertheless,
the acquisition will allow us to continue offering the readers of our
publications the widest range of photographs. When they appear in
publications, the photographs will be credited to Ships in Focus.

As we reach the end of another notional volume of *Record*,
we include an extra eight pages, four of which are devoted to an
index of ships and articles in issues 25 to 28. Despite the additional
pages, we still have insufficient space for material scheduled for
publishing in this issue, and a follow-up on 'Renfrew Retrospective'
in *Record* 26 has had to be held over, along with several letters.

Those readers who like their *Records* bound should send
them to Ken Toft Bookbinders, Unit 4, Brassey Street (off Laird
Street), Birkenhead, CH41 8BY. The charge for binding each
volume is now £25 plus £4 postage.

John Clarkson   Roy Fenton

SUBSCRIPTION RATES FOR RECORD

Readers can start their subscription with *any* issue, and are welcome
to backdate it to receive previous issues.

	3 issues	4 issues
UK	£23	£31
Europe (airmail)	£25	£34
Rest of world (surface mail)	£25	£34
Rest of world (airmail)	£30	£40

On 10th July 1937 Basil Feilden photographed the maiden arrival on the Mersey of Delius, first of the D class with its highly unusual profile.

[J. and M. Clarkson]

194

Fleet in Focus
LAMPORT AND HOLT D CLASS

'I do want a fine ship. I want a ship that will look first class, that will behave first class, and one that will be a money-making ship with something unique about it'. In this way Harland and Wolff were briefed in 1936 by Philip Haldin, the managing director of Lamport and Holt Ltd.

Few companies needed their spirits lifted as much as Lamport and Holt. In almost a hundred years of existence, the liner company that had been founded by a member of the renowned Holt family had never been brought so low. One cause was the crash of the Kylsant empire, of which Lamport and Holt had been part since 1911, and whose financial ruin had been hastened by expensive re-equipment in the years immediately following the First World War. As part of the collapse, Lamport and Holt went into receivership in September 1930. The depression of the late 1920s and early 1930s also impacted particularly heavily on the company's services to South America. Morale at Lamport and Holt had also been depressed by the loss by fire in 1928 of the passenger ship *Vestris* whilst on the important New York to South America route, a service the company was subsequently forced to abandon. The result was that a fleet numbering 41 vessels in 1930 was reduced to 21 in 1938, and even the 20 not sold or scrapped had spent time laid up.

Sorting out the mess left after the Kylsant crash was described as 'like unscrambling eggs'. In 1934, once the claims arising from the *Vestris* tragedy had been paid, the remaining Lamport and Holt ships and the company's surviving goodwill was acquired by a new company, Lamport and Holt Ltd., financed by various shipping entrepreneurs including Haldin of Court Line and Philip Runciman.

The initial order to Harland and Wolff for three motor ships was to be a symbol of the company's resurgence, although the general economic recovery from the depression was no doubt apparent to Lamport and Holt's new owners. The company had previously built motor ships, the *Leighton* (7,412/1921), *Linnell* (7,424/1921) and *Lassell* (7,417/1922), but little of the design expertise could have remained, as Lamport and Holt had not taken delivery of a new ship since 1923. Indeed, the brief to Harland and Wolff suggests that the design was to be largely left to the builders.

LEIGHTON

Lamport and Holt's earliest motor ships were a trio from A. MacMillan and Son of Dumbarton which were engined by Harland and Wolff and driven by twin screws. Neat, cruiser-sterned, if rather conventional looking, they had a very short hatch immediately abaft of the superstructure, and lattice derricks. The Leighton (7,412/1921) was the only one to survive the Second World War. She was sold to breakers soon afterwards, but Smith and Houston Ltd. sold her on to the Government, who proceeded to fill her with chemical ammunition. She was scuttled 100 miles west of Malin Head on 9th August 1947.

Like several other companies, Lamport and Holt had sought to moderate the impact of the 1930s lay-ups on its sea staff by crewing one of Leighton's sisters, the Lassell, entirely with certificated officers. Commanding so many experienced men must have been a daunting experience for her master. That this accumulated expertise did not always make for trouble-free voyaging is apparent from reports of a voyage during which a typhoid epidemic cost two lives.

[J. and M . Clarkson]

Unique profile

The ship's unique feature was the combined funnel and superstructure, which gave an appearance not previously achieved in a British ship. Indeed, the company and builders made the most of it by having a waterline model made and photographed for use in press reports of the launch of *Delius* which appeared in April 1937. The funnel housed the wireless room, the radio officer's cabin, the captain's bedroom and part of the accommodation for 12 passengers. Harland and Wolff had put the forward funnel on the *Georgic* to much the same uses.

As the accompanying general arrangement drawing shows, the hull was divided into six holds rather than the five that were usual for a ship of the type. The cargo space was further divided by the three decks. Cargo gear comprised 18 derricks capable of fairly modest lifts of 5, 7 or 10 tons, and one 35-ton derrick serving the large number 3 hold. There was a fashion for cargo liners of the 1920s and 1930s to be fitted with heavy-lift derricks of much larger capacity, for instance the *City of Barcelona* (5,698/1930; see *Record* 19 page 181) *Mary Kingsley* (4,017/1930; see *Record* 27) and *Clan Macdougall* (6,843/1929), and the modest lifting capacity of the Lamport and Holt ships is surprising. They certainly were called upon to

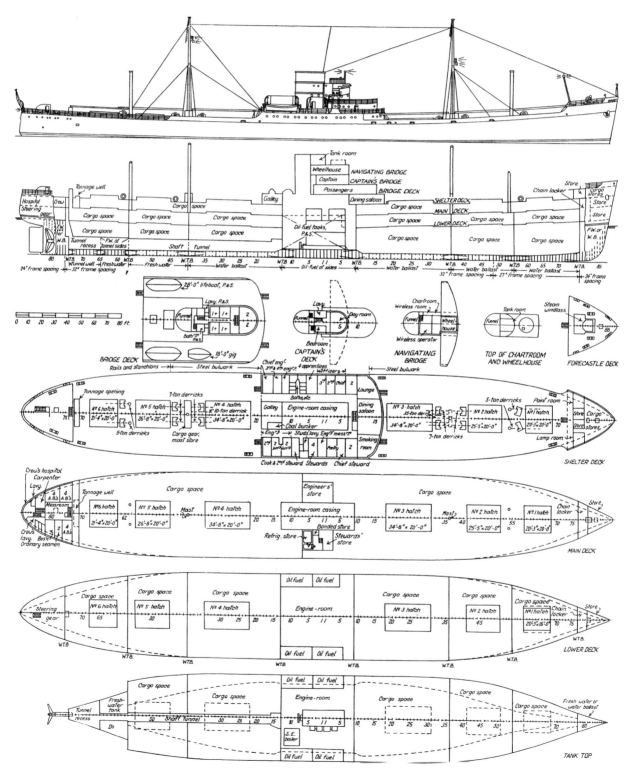

Fig. 2.—General Arrangement of the Lamport & Holt Motor-driven Cargo Liner "Delius."

ship heavy loads: a photograph from November 1938 shows a Mersey Docks and Harbour Board floating crane lifting on to *Delane* one of four 80-ton 4-6-0 locomotives built by Vulcan Foundry for the Buenos Ayres Great Southern Railway. Presumably the company felt there was sufficient heavy-lift craneage available at the major ports it served.

The main engine was a Harland-B&W type double-acting two-stroke with six cylinders. It propelled *Delius* at a sedate 12 knots. Also rather conservative was the specification of steam auxiliaries, including winches, all pumps, compressors to provide starting air for the diesel engines, and steering gear. The main boiler used waste heat from the exhaust gases from the engines supplemented by burning fuel oil. There were both steam and diesel generators to provide electricity for lighting and for the electric fans in each cabin, the one modest nod at improving comfort for crew and passengers in hot weather. The accommodation amidships was solely for officers and passengers: the crew were berthed in the poop. Only the ship's profile could therefore be considered innovative.

Expanding and developing the class

For the builders, chairman Frank Rebbeck gave the usual up-beat speech at the launch of *Delius* in April 1937, encouraging the owners to double their order to six 'before costs get any higher.' In fact, Harland and Wolff were losing money on these and most other ships they were building at the time: the losses on the second and third ships, *Delane* and *Devis,* were reported to be almost £27,000 on a contract price of £332,762. Replying, and noting Rebbeck's boast that Harland and Wolff had launched a greater tonnage than any other British yard in 1936, Philip Haldin hoped that the yard would achieve the same target in 1937, but noted that it would only do so if within the year it launched and completed *Delane* and *Devis* which his company badly needed. It would seem he was already aware of delays, and in the event these ships were not delivered until January and February 1938.

Lamport and Holt did order a further four ships to broadly the same design from Belfast, with detail differences that are apparent in the photos accompanying this feature. The *Defoe* and the *Debrett* were ordered during peacetime and delivered in 1940, the second *Devis* and the second *Defoe* were ordered later, not emerging until 1944 and 1945.

With developments to the design which saw later ships' speed increased to 13 or 14 knots and the 1945 *Defoe* emerge with a long bridge deck, Lamport and Holt seemed determined to perpetuate the design and give themselves a very distinctive fleet. However, their new owners were to have different ideas. In March 1944 a bid for the company from the Vestey Group was accepted by the majority of shareholders, and Lamport and Holt became effectively a subsidiary of Blue Star Line Ltd. One reason for directors' and shareholders' acceptance of the Vestey offer (Runciman had made an earlier, unsuccessful, bid) was that Lamport and Holt's South American services neatly fitted in with those of Blue Star, allowing some integration and rationalisation.

The Vestey take-over saw Lamport and Holt lose its recently-acquired independence of spirit, not least in terms of ship design. Although Lamport and Holt were to acquire a good many ships after the Second World War, only six full-sized cargo liners were actually built to their own design. Others were second-hand acquisitions, transfers from Blue Star or Booth, or were built to a standard design in the case of its four SD14s in the late 1970s. In addition there were coasters and reefers, the latter a type Lamport and Holt had not previously operated. The seven D class, therefore, represent a brief flowering of the company's spirit in the eight years in which it was an independent concern, between ownership by two large groups.

Service and fates

As the accompanying biographies set out, two of the seven Ds did not survive the war, one due to direct enemy action and one due to carrying dangerous war materials. Peacetime saw much integration of the Lamport and Holt, Blue Star and Booth fleets, with frequent transfers between them, sometimes with and sometimes without alterations to livery and name. In the mid-fifties the five surviving Ds were affected by such changes, when transferred to Blue Star and renamed for a service to the west coast of North America. After only a year they began returning to Lamport and Holt and reverting to their original names, in most cases resuming South American sailings.

The captions to the accompanying photographs explore the surprising number of variations in design and in-service modifications, which suggest that they should be referred to as the D group rather than the D class. Indeed, the five that survived for post-war service could quite readily be told apart thanks to these differences.

The Ds were not notably long-lived ships: Harland-B&W diesels were notorious for requiring more and more maintenance as they aged. The longest life of a D was 24 years, with the poor 1944-built *Devis* only managing 18. Four were sold outside the Vestey group, but for all except the second *Defoe,* which traded as *Argolis Star,* the new owners simply loaded the ships with scrap for a delivery voyage to breakers in the Far East.

With the D class Lamport and Holt Ltd. achieved their ambitions of creating distinctive and, one guesses, money-making ships. If the company had remained independent, perhaps a whole fleet built to this design might have appeared in post-war years. Instead its new owners had no need, or perhaps no desire, for such distinction. The combined funnel and superstructure was perpetuated on a few occasions by other builders and for other owners. Notable were the Sunderland-built sisters *Silverplane* and *Silverbriar* (both 7,226/1948) in which the forward funnel was a dummy containing accommodation (see *Record* 8), and examples of British and German motor coasters with the feature come to mind. Harland and Wolff created an idiosyncratic design, but not one that had a lasting influence.

Summary of dates and tonnages as built							
Name	Yard No	Launch	Delivery	Gross	Net	Sold	Lost/scrapped
Delius	980	12.4.37	6.7.37	6,065	3,749	1961	1962
Delane	1001	21.10.37	17.1.38	6,054	3,744	1961	1961
Devis (1)	1002	21.12.37	14.2.38	6,054	3,744	-	1943
Debrett	1029	20.3.40	23.5.40	6,244	3,796	1964	1964
Defoe (1)	1030	20.6.40	30.8.40	6,245	3,795	-	1942
*Devis** (2)	1181	12.4.44	20.8.44	8,187	5,771	1962	1962
*Defoe** (2)	1182	28.2.45	31.5.45	8,462	6,133	1966	1969
Dimensions were: 456 feet (oa) x 62.3 x 25.4 (33.9*) feet							

DELIUS and PORTLAND STAR

The photographs on this page show Delius launched on 12th April 1937 (right), on trials in early July (middle), and her first arrival in the Mersey on 10th July 1937 when caught by the camera of Basil Feilden (bottom). The last shows how the blue base of Lamport and Holt's funnel colours was carried forward on the superstructure. The structure below and ahead of the actual navigating bridge appears to be a docking bridge.

Delius's wartime adventures included participation in the Norwegian campaign in April 1940, when she was damaged by air attack, and during the evacuation of troops from Cherbourg and Bordeaux in June. Her greatest danger came during November 1943 in the Western Approaches when hits from radio-controlled bombs caused four deaths. Repairs may well have involved fitting the supports beneath the bridge wings which are apparent in the pre-war views opposite.
[Ulster Folk and Transport Museum 6107 and 8290; J. & M. Clarkson]

In the post-war view above, Delius looks rather drab without the distinctive waterline hull band. Gone is the continuation of the blue funnel colour on the superstructure. Additions to exhaust pipes now protrude from the funnel.

Transfer to Blue Star in April 1954 saw her become Portland Star and gain refrigeration equipment (right).

In 1958 she reverted to Delius. Note how in the 1959 photograph below the white upper strake and forecastle in the upper view quite alters the overall impression.

Delius was sold to become the Panamanian Kettara VII in June 1961, as which she made one voyage with scrap to Japan. She arrived at Tokyo in February 1962 and from there went to Izumi-Ohstu where breaking up by Sangyo Shinko K.K. began on 30th April 1962. [F.R. Sherlock; Ships in Focus (2)]

DELANE and SEATTLE STAR

The innovative profile of the Ds almost got Delane into trouble in December 1939. Heading into Montevideo, she was initially identified as a German cruiser by the British participants in the Battle of the River Plate.

A repeat of Delius, she did not have continuation of the blue funnel base forward on to her superstructure, as the pre-war Feilden view above demonstrates.

Delane was not given the extra supports to her bridge wings, so that in post-war years she was the only D to represent the original design (right).

Painting into Blue Star colours in April 1954 when she was renamed Seattle Star (below) altered her appearance markedly. Unlike other Ds, she did not revert to Lamport and Holt ownership, and remained

Seattle Star until June 1961. On sale to the same French owners who bought Delius she became the Panama-flagged Kettara VI, and proceeded east. She arrived at Hong Kong on 13th October, and on 27th

December breaking up commenced by Hong Kong Rolling Mills Ltd. [J. and M. Clarkson; J.K. Byass; Ships in Focus]

DEVIS (1)

Third of the original trio of Ds, the first *Devis* was launched on 21st July 1937 (top). She showed minor detail differences from *Delius,* including an enlarged monkey island, whilst she lacked the blue paint on the superstructure. This is noticeable in the middle photograph, taken by John MacRoberts in the Mersey on 21st May 1938: note the deck cargo of railway equipment.

The bottom photograph of *Devis* at Capetown was taken on 3rd September 1940, and little has been altered apart from the funnel colours being painted out and - possibly - a gun appearing on her stern.

Devis was lost in action on 5th July 1943: torpedoed by *U 593* when commodore ship of a convoy supporting the invasion of Sicily, and one of the mercifully few German submarine successes against this invasion fleet. None of *Devis's* crew were lost, but tragically 52 of the 289 Canadian troops on board were drowned before they could be rescued by HMS *Cleveland*. [Ulster Folk and Transport Museum 6553; J. & M. Clarkson; Ships in Focus]

DEBRETT and WASHINGTON STAR

In the second batch of Ds the superstructure was treated differently. The deckhouse immediately below the funnel casing was extended, but the most striking feature was how the funnel casing itself extends forward to take in the monkey island. The bridge front was given the same curve as the forward part of the casing. This can be seen in the trials photograph taken on 23rd May 1940 (top). In the bottom view on this page note how the black top and blue base to the funnel were extended right forward. This photograph was taken on the Mersey on 7th May 1946, and comparison with the middle view, at Capetown just six months earlier, shows how the wartime fittings were only gradually removed.

Comparison of the photographs above with those opposite show that *Debrett* was considerably modified in post war years. Two pairs of kingposts and associated winches were added, immediately forward and immediately aft of the superstructure (opposite top). This modification was

probably done when she was fitted with refrigeration equipment in 1947.

When *Debrett* became *Washington Star* in 1955 she was not formally transferred to Blue Star, but remained in nominal Lamport and Holt ownership (opposite middle). The transfer to the west coast USA service, for which she was renamed, was short-lived: in barely a year she reverted to the name *Debrett*.

The end of *Debrett's* career was

hastened by a fire in her engine room in April 1964, which forced her to divert into Recife whilst bound from Buenos Aires to Liverpool. She was sold to Greek owners and renamed *Ambasciata,* but this was merely for a voyage loaded with scrap for the Far East. She arrived at Osaka on 28th December 1964, and demolition began in the following month.

[Ulster Folk and Transport Museum 7390;
Ships in Focus (2); J. & M. Clarkson;
Tony Atkinson collection]

DEFOE (1)

Seen below at her launch on 20th June 1940, the first *Defoe,* a twin of *Debrett,* was the shortest-lived of the D group. Her loss on 24th September 1942 was not directly due to enemy action but to an explosion in drums of aircraft varnish which is reported to have blown her bows off. Considering she was also carrying drums of liquid chlorine it was very fortunate that she could be abandoned without loss of life. The accident happened south west of Rockall during a voyage from Manchester to Famagusta. *[Ulster Folk and Transport Museum 7437]*

DEVIS (2) and OAKLAND STAR

Later in the war Lamport and Holt were permitted to order two further examples of the Ds, and even to incorporate some modifications. In the second *Devis* masts replaced the forward and aftermost sets of kingposts and she had additional boats mounted ahead of the bridge wings (top, on trials 10th August 1944). After the war, additional kingposts were added fore and aft of her bridge as in *Debrett*, probably in 1948 when *Devis* was fitted with refrigeration equipment (middle). Renaming *Oakland Star*

in 1955 did not occasion transfer away from Lamport and Holt ownership (below, February 1957). She reverted to *Devis* later in 1957.

The only D to be sold directly from Lamport and Holt to a breaker, *Devis* was delivered to Cantieri Navali del Golfo at La Spezia on 4th July 1962. She was only 18 years old. Her engines are shown (right) before fitting.   [Ulster Folk & Transport Museum 9455 and 5289; Ships in Focus (2)]

DEFOE (2), GEELONG STAR and ARGOLIS STAR

The final D represented a major departure from the previous design, incorporating a long bridge deck. It showed that, even in wartime, builder and owner were interested in refining the design. As built *Defoe* had no kingposts and only masts, at the same positions as those on *Devis*. She also had the extra boats (top two photos, the second on trials, 31st May 1945)

Again, *Defoe* was subjected to modifications. An extra set of kingposts can be seen ahead of the bridge in the lower middle photograph of her after the 1954 transfer to Blue Star as *Geelong Star* (the only D to receive a name not associated with the west coast of North America). In 1958 she reverted to *Defoe* but not Lamport and Holt ownership.

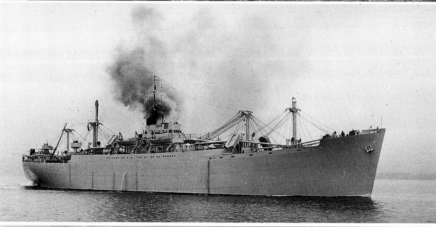

Defoe was the only D to make more than one voyage for an outside owner. In February 1966 she was sold for £135,000 to a London-Greek shipowner, Platon B. Metaxas. His Phoenix Shipping Co. Ltd. managed her on behalf of the Panama-based Astrofeliz Compania Naviera S.A. as the Greek-registered *Argolis Star* (bottom). A change of mind, or possibly of taxation regime, saw her move to the Greek-based Argolis Shipping Co. S.A. in 1967. The photograph of *Argolis Star* shows that at some time the pair of kingposts aft of the bridge had been removed.

The last voyage of a D group ship began when *Argolis Star* left Singapore on 17th October 1969. Twelve days later she was reported at Shanghai awaiting demolition.

[Roy Fenton collection; Ulster Folk and Transport Museum 9462; World Ship Photo Library collection; J. & M. Clarkson]

FONTEINS TO SOUTH AFRICA: Part 1
Peter Newall

The Netherlands has a long association with South Africa. In 1652 the Vereenigde Oostindische Compagnie (Dutch East India Company) created a refreshment station for its ships at the Cape and for the next 150 years the Cape colony was under Dutch rule. After the arrival of the British in 1806 many of the Dutch-speaking inhabitants known as Boers (farmers) moved north and eventually established their own republics in the Orange Free State and the Transvaal. Fiercely independent and with their own language Afrikaans, a form of Dutch, the Boers took on the might of the British Empire and were eventually defeated in 1900 in one of the bloodiest campaigns ever undertaken by Britain. Throughout the war, Holland supported the Boers and it is probably the main reason why there were no regular cargo and passenger services between Holland and South Africa until well after the Union of South Africa was formed in 1910.

This Holland Zuid-Afrika Lijn postcard was sent from *Klipfontein* (1) in July 1924. *[Peter Newall collection]*

At the end of September 1919 a Rotterdam-based company N.V. Van der Eb & Dresselhuys' Scheepvaart Maatschappij sent its *Mont Blanc* (2,031/1916) on a trial trip to South Africa. The success of this voyage led to the formation on 19th November 1919 of the N.V. Nederlandsche Zuid-Afrikaansche Stoomvaart Maatschappij (NZASM) by N.V. Van der Eb & Dresselhuys' Scheepvaart Maatschappij and another Rotterdam firm N.V. Furness' Scheepvaart en Agentuur Maatschappij, which had once been part of the British Furness shipping empire. Until it had its own fleet, the new service was operated with chartered tonnage. *Rijndijk* (3,557/1915) took the inaugural departure on 9th December 1919 when she left Rotterdam bound for East London, South Africa. A regular monthly service started on 20th November 1920 under the Holland Zuid-Afrika-Lijn name. By now the company had bought its first two ships *Bloemfontein* and *Jagersfontein*, both named after South African places ending in *-fontein* (fountain). The ships were given grey hulls and black funnels and, to emphasise the South African connection, the houseflag featured a springbok's head with the motto of the Union of South Africa *Eendracht maakt macht* (union is strength).

Bloemfontein started life in 1899 as *Anversville*, one of two sisters ordered by Elder Dempster for the African Steamship Company, but transferred on completion to its Belgium subsidiary Compagnie Belge Maritime du Congo S.A. In 1915 she sank after a fire off Nigeria but was later raised and towed to Lagos where she remained for the rest of the war. NZASM bought her from the British Government in 1920 and she was sent to Goole for repairs. With a dining room forward on the promenade deck, she carried over 140 passengers but was too small for the trade and was sold to Singapore buyers after only four years service. On the other hand,

Opposite: Holland-Afrika Lijn's last passenger ship, *Randfontein* (2) leaving Cape Town in 1959. *[Albert Newall]*
Above: The cargo-only *Jagersfontein* (1) was completed at Osaka in 1918. *[Gerrit de Boer collection]*

Rietfontein was a sister ship of *Jagersfontein* (1), but was fitted with accommodation for 30 passengers. *[Gerrit de Boer collection]*

Jagersfontein and the two vessels which joined the fleet in 1921, *Rietfontein* and *Randfontein*, were relatively new cargo ships. *Jagersfontein* and *Rietfontein* were both Japanese-built, standard-type three-island ships of around 6,000gt whilst the similar-sized *Randfontein* had been built on the Clyde for the Norwegian firm Fearnley & Eger. Both *Rietfontein* and *Randfontein* were given accommodation for 30 passengers which included a dining saloon, smoking room and lounge which were apparently rather cramped. For some reason *Jagersfontein* remained a cargo-only ship and was the only *-fontein* ship which did not carry passengers.

A yearly subsidy for a period of five years was awarded to NZASM by the Dutch Government and in 1921 and 1922 two new 7,000gt ships were built, *Springfontein* and *Klipfontein*. Both had a 30-passenger capacity whilst the latter was the first Dutch-built ship in the fleet and the only one fitted with turbines. Meanwhile, in 1920 eight of the leading Dutch shipping lines formed N.V. Vereenigde Nederlandsche Scheepvaart Maatschappij (The United Netherlands Company), The Hague to take over the cargo routes to Africa and Australasia formerly operated by the German

lines which had surrendered their fleets under the terms of the Treaty of Versailles. The German companies, however, made a remarkable come back and this caused major problems for the fledgling VNSM. Most of the VNSM ships had names ending in *-kerk* (church) and one of its routes was Holland-Oost-Afrika-Lijn, which served East African ports to Durban, via the Suez Canal.

Despite Government help, NZASM was soon in financial difficulties especially after the bankruptcy of N.V. Van der Eb & Dresselhuys' Scheepvaart Maatschappij. It was also unable to compete effectively with its main German rival Deutsche-Ost-Afrika-Linie which was building an outstanding group of passenger-cargo ships for its round-Africa service. In 1924, it was decided that NZASM would be managed by VNSM and that NZASM and Holland-Oost-Afrika-Lijn would operate a combined service to South and East Africa called Holland-Afrika Lijn. Most of Holland-Oost-Afrika Lijn's *-kerk* ships had limited passenger accommodation although in 1929 *Nieuwkerk* was completed with space for 52 passengers in first class only. The final blow for NZASM was the onset of the Great Depression and in September 1932 the firm went into

The brand-new *Springfontein* in 1921 painted in the original NZASM colours. *[Peter Newall collection]*

Jagersfontein (2), the second of Holland-Afrika Lijn's fast motorships of the 1930s, was torpedoed and sunk in 1942. *[Gerrit de Boer collection]*

liquidation and its ships and routes were absorbed into VNSM.

Under the Holland-Afrika Lijn banner the former NZASM ships were given the distinctive black funnel and single orange band colours of VNSM. The fleet also remained divided between those with -*fontein* names i.e. ships with larger numbers of passengers and the -*kerk* ones which were mainly cargo carriers. Not long after the merger, the company placed an order with the Amsterdam shipyard Nederlandsche Scheepsbouw Maatschappij for two 10,000gt passenger motor ships. Given that the world was still in the midst of a major financial crisis, this was a bold move. The sisters *Bloemfontein* and *Jagersfontein* took the names of the first two NZASM ships and carried 93 first class passengers in superb accommodation with all cabins featuring outside windows or portholes. The main public rooms on the promenade deck were very light and airy and included at the forward end was a palm court overlooking the bow, for relaxation and dancing. The single-sitting dining room was situated on the deck below and was also forward facing. Externally this pair were very distinctive but rather stiff looking with no rake to the funnel or masts. A curved Maierform bow gave them a service speed of over 16 knots and they were faster than any of the Deutsche-Ost-Afrika-Linie liners and most of the large Union-Castle Line mailships. *Bloemfontein* was also the first ship launched by long-distance wireless when General Hertzog, Prime Minister of South Africa, pressed a button at the Netherlands Legation in Pretoria at noon on the 16th June 1934. Meanwhile *Nieuwkerk* underwent an extraordinary conversion which included the replacement of her turbine engines with new diesels and the increase of her first class only passenger capacity from 52 to 88. She was also lengthened and fitted with a Maierform bow. Renamed *Boschfontein* she now had a service speed of 16 knots and joined *Bloemfontein* and *Jagersfontein* on Holland-Afrika Lijn's new express service to South and East Africa via Southampton.

The success of the new motor ships led to the

Boschfontein, seen here with Dutch neutrality markings, was a dramatic rebuild of the passenger-cargo freighter *Nieuwkerk.*
[Gerrit de Boer collection]

Klipfontein (2) sailing from Cape Town in July 1952. She was lost six months later off the Moçambique coast. *[Alex Duncan collection]*

order in 1937 for a trio of enlarged versions of *Bloemfontein* and *Jagersfontein* but with a raked bow instead of the Maierform one. *Klipfontein* and *Oranjefontein* were to be built at Rotterdam by Machinefabriek & Scheepswerf van P. Smit Jr., whilst *Elandsfontein* (laid down as *Rietfontein*) was to be constructed at Danzig by the F. Schichau G.m.b.H. Because Germany was short of hard currency, the German build was undertaken in exchange for Dutch tobacco. Not only were these new ships more powerful than their predecessors, they were also designed to carry 42 tourist class passengers in the poop. The 106 first class passengers meanwhile occupied the entire superstructure amidships in this unusual accommodation layout. Once again the main first class public rooms on the promenade deck were attractively designed with large windows arranged to offer passengers a clear view of the sea. They also had a permanent swimming pool for first class whereas on the earlier pair the pool was a canvas affair erected over No. 4 hatch. Spacious holds included insulated space for fruit and other produce. The two forward and two aft holds were worked with derricks whilst the remaining two fore and aft on the promenade decks had cranes. This was the same working arrangement as *Bloemfontein* and *Jagersfontein*.

Klipfontein was the first of the new liners to be completed and she made her maiden arrival at Cape Town on 4th September 1939, the day after war was declared between Britain and Germany. At that time Holland was a neutral country and all four motor ships were sent to the Far East on charter to the Java-Pacific Line. Despite its neutrality, the Netherlands was invaded on 10th May 1940 and soon afterwards all the *-fontein* ships were handed over to the Nederlandsche Scheepvaart en Handelscommissie (Netherlands Shipping and Trading Committee) which was the custodian of the merchant fleet for the Dutch Government in exile. In 1942 *Bloemfontein, Klipfontein* and *Boschfontein* were chartered to the US Navy as transports. Based in San Francisco, they spent much of the war years in the Pacific

and took part in many of the major campaigns against Japan. Also in 1942, *Jagersfontein* was torpedoed and sunk in the Atlantic, fortunately with no loss of life.

Meanwhile, *Oranjefontein,* which had been completed at the end of 1940, was seized by the Germans but survived the war more or less intact. In the Baltic, *Elandsfontein* was not so lucky. She was launched in March 1940 but after the invasion of the Netherlands work ceased. Ironically, the management of the semi-completed ship and *Oranjefontein* was awarded to Holland-Afrika Lijn's major rival, Deutsche-Ost-Afrika-Linie. In 1945 *Elandsfontein* was sunk in the River Vistula by the Russian Army during the battle for control of Germany's eastern territories. Two years later the wreck was raised and, after negotiations with the Russian Government, she was released and towed back to Holland for rebuilding. Thus in 1950, renamed in honour of the ship lost during the war and ten years after she was launched, *Jagersfontein* was finally completed. In the meantime the monthly South African service had recommenced early in 1946 with *Nijkerk* followed by *Randfontein* and *Oranjefontein* on her maiden voyage. In 1947 *Bloemfontein* was rebuilt and her superstructure extended aft of the mainmast. Her passenger capacity increased to 177 and for the first time she carried tourist class passengers. During the 1930s she was essentially a first class only ship apart from space in the bow for steerage passengers. The post-war passenger schedule was finally underway when *Jagersfontein* entered service in March 1950. Incidentally, she differed from her sisters in having derrick posts forward instead of cranes.

At 1.10 in the afternoon of 8th January 1953 tragedy struck *Klipfontein*. Whilst racing Union-Castle Line's *Bloemfontein Castle* (18,400/1949) for the sole berth at Beira, Moçambique she hit uncharted rocks five miles from the coast. Despite an explosion in the forepeak oil bunker, passengers had sufficient time to get into the lifeboats. Fortunately the weather was also calm and within 30 minutes *Bloemfontein Castle* arrived at the scene and rescued all passengers and crew. The ship sank at 4.20pm. The loss of *Klipfontein* was a major blow to Holland-Afrika Lijn but led to a replacement order for the finest of all the *-fontein* ships, the 13,694gt *Randfontein*. This beautifully proportioned ship was built in Holland by the Wilton-Fijnoord yard at Schiedam. With a service speed of over 18 knots, she was not only the fastest-ever Holland-Afrika liner, but also the first to carry more tourist class passengers than first. She entered service in January 1959 and replaced *Bloemfontein,* which was sold for scrap later that year. The 1960s were a period of great change on the Europe-South Africa run with increased competition from the new Union-Castle Line mailships and the gradual move away from sea to travel by air. On 23rd October 1965 *Randfontein* departed from Amsterdam on the one thousandth sailing for the Holland-Afrika Lijn since the Second World War.

In 1967 both *Oranjefontein* and *Jagersfontein* were withdrawn leaving *Randfontein* as the sole Holland-Afrika Lijn passenger liner. Two fast freighters, *Serooskerk* (9,821/1961) and *Simonskerk* (9,820/1960), each with limited accommodation for 12 passengers, took their place on the South African run. Three years later, on 1st July 1970, most of the major Dutch shipping lines including VNSM became part of a new Dutch shipping giant, Koninklijke Nedlloyd N.V. In the inevitable rationalisation which followed, it was announced that *Randfontein* would be transferred from the South African service to the Hong Kong-Australia route of Koninklijke Java-China Paketvaart Lijnen N.V. *Randfontein* brought to a close over 50 years of *-fontein* ships when she arrived at Rotterdam from South Africa on 3rd September 1971. By the end of the decade, most of the *-kerk* names had been replaced by dull corporate names beginning with *Nedlloyd*, thus finally bringing down the curtain on a great era of Dutch shipping.

Many thanks to Andrew Bell and the leading Dutch shipping historian Gerrit de Boer for their help with this story.
To be concluded with a fleet list and many more photographs.

Jagersfontein (3), was finally completed in 1950. Note the derrick posts forward. *[Ian Farquhar collection]*

The last and probably the finest of the company's ships, *Randfontein* (2) of 1959 at the yard of Wilton-Fijnoord, Schiedam.

[Peter Newall collection]

MIGRANTS AND BUTTER – THE FINLAND LINE TO HULL
Anthony Cooke

This article was sparked off by a remark made by a Finnish-American friend: 'Many people dreaming about America left Finland on a ship called *Titania* from Hanko to Hull, and then on another ship to New York. That was the way my Great Uncle David came over here.' That must have been before the First World War, as the *Titania* was sunk in 1918. She belonged to the Finland Steamship Company (called in Finnish, Suomen Höyrylaiva OY; and, to Swedish-speaking Finns, Finska Ångfartygs Aktiebolaget).

The Finland Line was not alone in running services from the Baltic to British ports. For many years, one of the main cargoes on these routes was butter in casks and some ships also carried passengers - in particular, migrants, many of whom were then transhipped to the vessels of the big Atlantic lines. (These passengers en route to America were called transmigrants.) The Wilson Line, for instance, brought large numbers into Hull. Many of them were then sent by train to Liverpool, where they were crowded into the Cunarders and other liners which would take them to America. Lassman Brothers, acting for the DFDS company of Copenhagen, ran a service between St. Petersburg and London. Competition for the migrant business also came from DFDS itself, which had a feeder route from Baltic ports to Copenhagen, where passengers were transferred to its Scandinavian-American Line ships. And, in later years, the new Swedish American Line also set up a feeder service, in this case to Gothenburg. In addition, the powerful Hamburg America Line was involved in the trade and, by the early years of the twentieth century, there were direct sailings from Baltic ports to New York by the Danish-owned Russian American Line.

Of course, some migrants coming into British ports stayed here. East European Jewish communities, for instance, grew up in such areas as Whitechapel in the East End of London, parts of Leeds and Manchester and in Hull

itself. But for most of the migrants landing in Britain, this country was merely a staging post on their journey through the 'Golden Door' into America. Many of those travelling on Finland Line ships were probably rather different from those on the vessels sailing from the other side of the Baltic - fair-haired Lutheran peasants, rather than refugees from the Jewish Pale escaping from the pogroms of successive Tsars. In all, the Finland Line is said to have carried 319,083 migrants out of Finnish ports between 1891 and 1924. Hanko, on the southernmost tip of the country's coastline, became an important port of embarkation for the emigrant trade.

Origins of the company
The Finland Steamship Company, for many years managed by members of the Krogius family of Helsinki, had been established in 1883 and took delivery of its first vessel, the *Sirius* (1,085gt) in the following year. She was a freighter but had cabin accommodation for nine passengers, as did her running mate, the *Orion* (also 1884/1,085). Both ships were placed on a route between Helsinki and Hull. By 1891, the company already had a fleet of eight freighters and it was in that year that it took delivery of its first fully-fledged passenger and mail steamers. The *Astraea* (1,118 gross tons) and the *Urania* (1,110 gross tons) came from the Neptune yard of Wigham Richardson and Co. on the Tyne. Single-screw ships powered by triple-expansion engines, they had cabin capacity for limited numbers of first and second class passengers but, equally importantly, they could carry up to 186 third class emigrants in the 'tweendecks and in dormitories at the stern. (Passengers in the higher classes were accommodated amidships, well away from the noise and vibration of the propeller.) Both ships were fitted with the new electric lighting. Finland being then a Grand Duchy within Imperial Russia, they flew the Russian flag. It is

Titania of 1908 in the Humber. [Barnard and Straker/J. and M. Clarkson]

Arcturus of 1908 passes beneath the Levensau Bridge on the Kiel Canal. *[Laurence Dunn collection]*

known that some services maintained by Russian-owned vessels received financial aid from the government - whether this was extended to Finnish-owned ships is not certain.

As the nineteenth century drew to a close, the Finland Line began to develop other routes. In particular, in 1892 it acquired several second-hand steamers which it employed in a service from St. Petersburg to Stockholm via Helsinki, Hanko, Turku (sometimes) and Mariehamn in the Åland Islands. For a time, this became the company's busiest route but there were also sailings from St. Petersburg to Stettin via Helsinki. This route, too, carried emigrants. Rail connections between St. Petersburg and Moscow were advertised. A network of cargo-only services was also developed, stretching out to Bremen, Hamburg, Middlesbrough, Newcastle, Antwerp, Dunkirk, Le Havre, Bordeaux, Spanish and Portuguese ports and Marseilles. But it is the ships sailing to Hull which concern us here.

A new and larger passenger vessel was brought into the service in late 1898, the *Arcturus* (2,017gt). One of several ships delivered to the company over the next decade by Gourlay Bros. of Dundee, she had a three-cylinder triple-expansion engine considerably more powerful than the units in the earlier vessels. She was followed in 1899 by a near-sister, the *Polaris* (2,017gt). Both ships could accommodate 80 first class passengers in ornate, mahogany-panelled comfort. The *Arcturus* could also carry 185 third class passengers and the *Polaris* 160. Both were obviously very strongly built and, indeed, the *Arcturus* survived for 59 years, until 1957. (The Finland Line tended to hold onto good ships, whatever their age; and, in addition, the careers of several of its vessels were almost certainly prolonged by the massive problems which it faced after the Second World War.)

By 1899, the company had a fleet of 31 ships, mainly small freighters. In 1908, the line took delivery of its biggest and finest passenger ship yet, the famous but relatively short-lived *Titania* (3,463gt). She too came from the Gourlay yard and could carry 86 first class passengers in Edwardian-style luxury, 68 second class and no less than 585 third - an indication of how the line's migrant trade had developed. These third class travellers now all slept in large dormitories. *Titania* was equipped with refrigeration machinery and by now 'Lloyd's Register' was also shewing

Arcturus and *Polaris* as having been fitted with it.

A 1910 advertisement in 'Bradshaw's General Railway and Steam Navigation Guide for Great Britain and Ireland' offered a sailing every Wednesday from Hull to Copenhagen and Hanko (Hango) either by the *Titania* or the *Arcturus;* and a similar service every Saturday to Copenhagen and Åbo (i.e. Turku) by the *Polaris* and *Astraea*. Passengers were only carried to Helsinki (Helsingfors) during the ice-free summer months but the company had for some years been competing in the Copenhagen trade. Through tickets could thus be offered from Hull to Stockholm via Copenhagen; and they were also available to St. Petersburg via the Finnish ports. The *Urania* was presumably by now sailing on other routes or was perhaps being kept as a reserve ship. In any case, she was lost in February 1913 after colliding with the steamer *Fancy* of Tønsberg in Norway. She was replaced almost immediately by another *Urania* (1,934gt), bought second-hand from the French company Société Générale de Transports Maritimes à Vapeur. As their *Russie*, she had been built at Sunderland in 1897. With accommodation for 102 first class passengers, 48 second and, importantly, 450 third, she was obviously deemed to be suitable for the Hull service.

Both the second *Urania* and the *Titania* were lost during the First World War. When war broke out in August 1914, they were trapped at Hull, unable to return home since, with Czarist Russia on the Allied side, they would have had to run the gauntlet of German naval power in the North Sea and the Baltic. Eventually, the *Urania* was chartered to the Imperial Russian government but struck a mine in the White Sea in July 1915 while on a voyage from Liverpool to Archangel. Later, the British Admiralty took over the *Titania*, renamed her *Tithonus* and used her as an armed boarding steamer patrolling the waters off the coast of Scotland. She too sank in March 1918. Different sources claim either that she hit a mine or that she was the victim of a submarine. The *Polaris* was also lost to the company, being requisitioned by the Russian government and never returned after the Revolution.

Independence for Finland
The First World War sparked off seismic changes in Finland.

An independence movement had been active for some years and it now sought support from the German government. In fact, many volunteers fought on the German side. The Russian Revolution gave the patriots their opportunity and Finland was declared an independent nation on the 6th December 1917. But almost immediately, fighting erupted between the patriots and left-wing elements who favoured rule by the new Bolshevik regime in Russia. Ships of the Finland Line played an important part in this Civil War, carrying a patriot battalion, which had been fighting alongside the Germans, back across the Baltic from Libau in February 1918. It was a dangerous voyage through ice- and mine-infested waters and the *Arcturus,* in particular, performed heroically, bringing back 940 men and large quantities of ammunition despite colliding with the ice-breaker *Sampo,* which was accompanying her. The *Sampo* had only recently escaped from seizure by the Russian Navy. Both ships flew the flag of the new Finland and were greeted by cheering crowds. The *Arcturus* then made further voyages, bringing soldiers over from Danzig. In the end, the patriotic forces were victorious and Finnish independence was secured.

Within months of the end of the First World War, the Hull cargo/passenger service was resumed by the *Arcturus* and the *Astræa.* But things had changed. The political upheavals in the Baltic area may have altered the pattern of trade and, certainly, the company had lost many of its ships. Furthermore, the imposition by Congress in 1921, 1924 and 1929 of progressively more severe quotas on immigration into the United States affected the passenger business on the route. Nevertheless, the Hull ships continued to carry passengers, now with the emphasis on business travellers and tourists. Ever since the early years of the century, John Good and Sons Ltd., the company's British agents, had been advertising the service under the slogan, 'Off The Beaten Track'. They now commissioned Harry Hudson Rodmell (who also worked for several other shipping companies, including the Bergen Line) to design colourful and attractive posters and brochures, which have since become collectors' items. They beautifully preserve the memory of those rather staid-looking Finnish ships with their white hulls and severely upright, rim-topped black funnels adorned with two narrow white bands. The apt and enticing 'Off The Beaten Track' slogan continued to be featured until the outbreak of another World War in 1939.

The *Arcturus* and *Astræa* were assisted at times by the *Ariadne* (1914/2,558), another enduring ship - she survived in the company's fleet until 1969. She had been built in Sweden for the Stettin service but over the years served on most of the Finland Line's passenger routes. It would seem from photographs that her first class interiors were particularly attractive, in what became known as the National Romantic style. They were notable for their large expanses of plain but highly polished wood panelling. The *Ariadne* was intended for use mainly during the summer months and so she differed from many of her fleetmates in not being fully strengthened for navigation through ice.

New ships for the Hull service
It was not until 1925 that the company was once again able to take delivery of a new ship specifically built for the Hull service. The *Oberon* - alas, there was no longer a *Titania* to act as a running-mate - was built in France by the Penhoët company, but at Rouen rather than at their famous St. Nazaire yard. Fitting out,

however, was sub-contracted to Earle's at Hull. In most respects, the *Oberon* (3,008gt) was a very traditional Finland Line ship: she had an ice-breaker bow, a wooden bridge-front, a tall, vertical funnel and a counter stern; and her old-fashioned triple-expansion engine drove a single screw. Her furnaces, though, were oil-fired; and her first class interiors were considered very modern in 1925. She was the last of the Hull line steamers to make sizeable provision for third class passengers. Unfortunately, she had a very brief life, sinking after colliding with the *Arcturus* in the Kattegat on a foggy day in December 1930. She sank in only 4½ minutes and only 37 of her 61 crew and 4 of the 21 passengers were saved.

Tragically the masters of the two ships were brothers: Captain Eric Hjelt was in command of the *Oberon* and Captain Ossi Hjelt was in charge of the *Arcturus.* As the *Oberon* would be away from home over Christmas, Captain Eric Hjelt had taken his wife and family along for the trip. So had the Second officer and the First Engineer. Captain Eric Hjelt's wife and daughter were among those who lost their lives. By coincidence, the Finnish-American friend whose stray remark about her uncle prompted me to write this article, also had a relation by marriage on the *Oberon* that fateful day. Thanks to a series of what she described as 'miracles', she was one of the survivors.

The Great Depression, of course, had its effect on the Hull service and an advertisement in the January 1935 Bradshaw shews that it had been reduced to a single weekly sailing in each direction, every Wednesday. Perhaps because of the collapse of the emigrant trade, Hanko and Turku were no longer included in the schedule and the Finnish terminal port was now Helsinki (still referred to as Helsingfors). Connections were offered to Tallinn and to Leningrad, as St. Petersburg was then known. Two ships maintained the service, the faithful *Arcturus* and the *Ilmatar.*

The *Ilmatar* (2,365gt) had been completed in 1929 by Burmeister & Wain of Copenhagen. Burmeisters were, of course, famous for their pioneering work on the marine diesel engine, but the Finland Line had specified a triple-expansion steam engine. Long experience of the reliability and simplicity of this type of engine seems to have made them reluctant to change. And, having flirted with oil-fired furnaces on the *Oberon,* they now reverted to coal. The *Ilmatar* was built for service between Helsinki, Tallinn and Stettin and between Helsinki and Lübeck, but became a stalwart of the Hull route. She had an elder sister, slightly smaller, which also appeared on the Hull route, the *Wellamo* (1927/2,047). She, too, was a Burmeister & Wain product. Both sisters had the reputation of being comfortable ships, even though they lacked the *Oberon's* chic.

Another addition to the passenger fleet between the two wars was the second *Polaris* (1912/1,615). When they bought her in 1933, the Finland Line must already have been

Ilmatar of 1928. *[Laurence Dunn collection]*

Aallotar of 1937. *[Laurence Dunn collection]*

very familiar with her since they had seen her sailing in and out of Stettin for many years. She had been built there as the *Prinzessin Sophie Charlotte* for the local Neue Dampfer-Compagnie, becoming the *Preussen* after the war when, with the collapse of the monarchy, royal names were no longer acceptable in Germany. Already into middle age when she joined the Finland Line fleet, she had a very traditional appearance, complete with 'Woodbine' funnel. Her new owners had her fitted with refrigeration machinery and used her for North Sea service, mainly to Antwerp but sometimes to Hull and, latterly, to London where she berthed in the Surrey Commercial Docks. A somewhat slower ship than some of her Finland Line fleetmates, she was probably bought mainly as a cargo-carrier but she did have berths for 60 first class and 18 second class passengers.

A more imposing ship came into service in 1936, when the company took delivery of the *Aallotar* (2,916gt). She was another Danish-built vessel, but this time from the Helsingør yard. While remaining loyal to steam, the Finland Line had specified a four-cylinder compound engine of a more modern type for their new ship. Some concessions to modernity were also made in her appearance - a raked bow and a steel bridge-front - but she still had a counter stern. With a capacity for 97 first class passengers and 84 second, she was placed on the Hull route.

It will be apparent that at a time when other companies operating across the North Sea were introducing successively bigger, faster and more modern mini-liners, the Finland Line chose not to enter the race but continued to use fairly modest ships. They clearly felt that traffic from the eastern Baltic did not justify the construction of more pretentious vessels. They were not alone in this - the state-owned Russian service between Leningrad and London was maintained by rather crude motorships with a service speed of just 12 knots. But the Finland Line ships, though small, were much superior and they had a fine reputation for quiet comfort. They acquired a good following, particularly among tourist passengers.

By 1939, the company had another passenger/ cargo ship on order - the *Astrea*, which was to be of about 3,000 tons. Unusually, she was being built at home in Finland - at the Crichton-Vulkan yard at Turku - and she was diesel powered. She was launched shortly after the outbreak of the Second World War, by which time the North Sea service, for which she was intended, had necessarily been suspended. The following year, the still incomplete ship was damaged by bombing. (Although Finland maintained a precarious neutrality, parts of the country had been invaded by the Russians, while German forces had been given access to other areas.) Most of the Finland Line's passenger ships had been laid up and only on the route to Stockholm, in neutral Sweden, was it possible to maintain anything more than a minimal service. In 1944, damaged and still unfinished, the *Astrea* was sold to the Svea Line of Stockholm. The story of how the Swedish company had reached a secret agreement with the Bergen Line to complete the ship and then to sell her on to the Norwegians once the War was over, has been told in the article on the Bergen Line in *Ships In Focus Record 22*. Suffice it here to say that, still under the name *Astrea*, she helped to re-establish her new owners' Bergen–Tyne service in the immediate post-war years.

War ends the service

The Second World War proved to be even more costly to the Finland Line than the First had been. Not only had large parts of Finland been fought over but the country was forced to pay huge war reparations to Russia. Part of these payments was made in the form of ships and the Finland Steamship Company was stripped of 23 vessels, including some of its best. Of the passenger ships, the *Ilmatar*, the *Aallotar*, the *Polaris* and the *Ariadne* were all to be handed over. In the event, the *Ariadne* never passed into Russian hands since she ran seriously aground while being delivered to the Soviets. The company regained possession and, although she was now over thirty years old, spent a great deal of money on lengthening and restoring her.

The cargo/passenger service to Hull was never resumed. Instead, the *Arcturus* ran between Helsinki and Antwerp but increasingly the company concentrated on the Baltic routes to Sweden, Germany and Denmark. Some of these services were run jointly with the Bore and Svea companies and eventually became the Silja Line, famous operators of some of the biggest and most spectacular ferries ever known - a far cry from the modest Finland Line vessels of the pre-war era. The Finland Steamship Company itself became known as EFFOA but the ships still sported the well-known black funnel livery with two white bands. The fleet included a number of sizeable bulk-carriers and ro-ros. In 1990, EFFOA merged with the Johnson Line of Sweden, under the hybrid name Effjohn.

As for the passenger link between Finland and Britain, it was left to the Russians, the Baltic Steamship Company, to provide a call at Helsinki on their Leningrad –UK service. One of the ships used was the *Beloostrov*, once the *Aallotar*, the pride of the Finland Line.

Fleet list of vessels used regularly on the Hull route

SIRIUS 1884-1918
1,085g 809n 209.9 (bp) x 30.0 x 14.6 feet.
C.2-cyl. by Gute Hoffnungshütte, Sterkrade; 99 NHP. Single screw.
3.1884: Completed by Bremer Schiffbau, Vegesack (Yard No. 107) for Finska Ångfartygs A/B.
3.1918: Taken over by the Shipping Controller and transferred to London registry under the management of Gellatly, Hankey and Co.
29.6.1918: Sunk by an internal explosion, 1½ miles west by south of Longships Lighthouse while on a voyage from Penarth with a cargo of coal. Various accounts claim a mine and a German submarine were responsible, and war loss insurance was paid on the ship.

ORION 1884-1931
1,085g 805n 210.0 (bp) x 30.0 x 14.6 feet.
C.2-cyl. by Gute Hoffnungshütte, Sterkrade; 101 NHP. Single screw.
5.1884: Completed by Bremer Schiffbau, Vegesack for Finska Ångfartygs A/B.
28.12.1931: Wrecked at Gråskärsbådarne outside Helsinki at the end of a voyage from Rouen with general cargo.

URANIA (1) 1891-1913
1,110g 706n 220.0 (bp) x 32.0 x 12.7 feet.
T.3-cyl. by Wigham Richardson and Co., Newcastle-upon-Tyne; 253 NHP. Single screw.
8.1891: Completed by Wigham Richardson and Co., Newcastle-upon-Tyne (Yard No. 267) for Finska Ångfartygs A/B.
3.2.1913: Sank after a collision in fog north west of Kullen in the Kattegat with the Norwegian steamer FANCY (1,613/1883) whilst on a voyage from Hull to Copenhagen with coal and general cargo. Crew and passengers landed at Elsinore.

ASTRÆA 1891-1930
1,118g 662n 220.0 (bp) x 32.0 x 12.7 feet.
T.3-cyl. by Wigham Richardson and Co., Newcastle-upon-Tyne; 253 NHP. Single screw.
9.1891: Completed by Wigham Richardson and Co., Newcastle-upon-Tyne (Yard No. 268) for Finska Ångfartygs A/B.
4.10.1920: Ran aground on the island of Skaw but refloated.
20.2.1930: Sold to H. A. Elfving, Hanko and used as a mother ship for his fishing fleet.
18.6.1934: Transferred to Elfvingin Kalastuslaivue OY.
15.7.1936: Sold to Thomas Young, Sunderland for breaking up.
10.1936: Delivered.

ARCTURUS 1898-1957
2,017g 1,136n 281.4 (bp) x 38.2 x 13.7 feet.
T.3-cyl. by Gourlay Brothers and Co., Dundee; 535 NHP. Single screw.
12.1898: Completed by Gourlay Brothers and Co., Dundee (Yard No. 183) for Finska Ångfartygs A/B.
1914: Laid up at Stockholm.
2.1918: Played a prominent part in the transport of military units back to Finland to participate in the Civil War.
19.12.1930: Collided with the company's OBERON in the Kattegat.
7.5.1957: Arrived at Hendrik-Ido-Ambacht to be broken up by Holland Scheepswerf en Machinehandel.

POLARIS (I) 1899-1915
2,011g 1,150n 281.4 (bp) x 38.2 x 13.7 feet.
T.3-cyl. by Gourlay Brothers and Co., Dundee; 535 NHP. Single screw.
3.1899: Completed by Gourlay Brothers and Co., Dundee (Yard No. 184) for Finska Ångfartygs A/B.
4.1915: Requisitioned by the Imperial Russian Government and served as an accommodation ship at Helsinki as KRETCHET. Later allocated to Sovtorgflot, at Odessa and later Vladivostok.
25.12.1941: Sunk in Japanese air attack whilst lying in Hong Kong harbour. Wreck removed and broken up after the war.

TITANIA 1908-1918
3,463g 1,933n 330.0 (bp) x 44.8 x 23.6 feet.

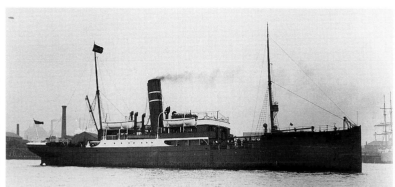
Urania (1) of 1891. *[Barnard and Straker/J. and M. Clarkson]*

Arcturus. [Laurence Dunn collection]

Polaris. [Barnard and Straker/J. and M. Clarkson]

Titania. [Barnard and Straker/Laurence Dunn collection]

T.3-cyl. by Gourlay Brothers and Co., Dundee; 658 NHP. Single screw.
8.1908: Completed by Gourlay Brothers and Co., Dundee (Yard No. 228) for Finska Ångfartygs A/B.
8.1914: Laid up at Hull.
3.1916: Taken over by the British Admiralty, renamed HMS TITHONUS.
28.3.1918: Torpedoed about 50 miles east of Aberdeen in position 57.04 north by 00.33 west by the German submarine UB 72 whilst escorting a convoy to Norway. There were four casualties.

Left: *Urania* (2). She was photographed on the Humber during her brief service for Finska Ångfartygs A/B. Bought from French owners in May 1913, in July she was sent to Earles at Hull for rebuilding, emerging in December 1913. However, on the outbreak of the First World War in August 1914 she was laid up at Hull and never resumed FAA service. *[Barnard and Straker/J. and M. Clarkson]*

Below: *Ariadne* following her post-war rebuild. *[Laurence Dunn collection]*

URANIA (2) 1913-1915

1,934g 746n 281.5 (bp) x 37.0 x 25.7 feet.
T.3-cyl. by North Eastern Marine Engineering Co. Ltd., Newcastle-upon-Tyne; 377 NHP. Single screw.
1897: Completed by Sunderland Shipbuilding Co., Sunderland (Yard No. 192) for Société Générale de Transports Maritimes à Vapeur, Marseilles as RUSSIE.
26.5.1913: Acquired by Finska Ångfartygs A/B, renamed URANIA and rebuilt by Earle's Shipbuilding and Engineering Co. Ltd., Hull.
8.1914: Laid up at Hull.
4.1915: Chartered to the Imperial Russian government.
14.7.1915: Sank after striking a mine south of Sviatoi Nos in the White Sea whilst on a voyage from Liverpool to Archangel with general cargo.

ARIADNE 1914-1969

2,558g 1,655n 258.0 (bp) x 43.7 x 18.9 feet.
T.3-cyl. by Lindholmens Varv., Gothenburg; 447 NHP. Single screw.
3.1914: Completed by Lindholmens Varv., Gothenburg (Yard No. 412) for Finska Ångfartygs A/B.
About 15.1.1945: Having been taken as war reparation by the USSR, she ran aground off Hamina during the delivery voyage and was not handed over.
10.1946 - 6.1948: Restored and lengthened (now 292 feet (oa), 280.0 (bp)).
1968: Laid up at Helsinki.
8.1969: Broken up by Helsingin Romuliike at Helsinki.

OBERON 1925-1930

3,008g 1,513n 291.0 (bp) x 44.1 x 21.4 feet.
T.3-cyl. by Chantiers et Ateliers de St. Nazaire (Penhoët), St. Nazaire; 655 NHP. Single screw.
8.1925: Completed, having been built by Chantiers et Ateliers de St. Nazaire (Penhoët), Rouen (Yard No. D5) and fitted out by Earle's Shipbuilding Co. Ltd., Hull for Finska Ångfartygs A/B.
19.12.1930: Collided with the company's ARCTURUS and sank in the Kattegat, seven miles south east of Laesö Trindel Lightvessel, while on a voyage from Helsinki to Hull.

The short-lived *Oberon* at Hull. *[Laurence Dunn collection]*

WELLAMO 1927-1967

2,047g 1,030n 262.4 (oa) x 50.5 x 39.8 x 22.4 feet.
T.3-cyl. by A/S Burmeister & Wain, Copenhagen; 364 NHP. Single screw.
6.1927: Completed by A/S Burmeister & Wain, Copenhagen for Finska Ångfartygs A/B.
19.12.1941: Suffered severe ice damage.
23.6.1967: Sold to M. Rauanheimo OY (A/B R. Nordström & Co., managers), Kokkola, Finland and renamed OULUTAR.
8.5.1969: Sold to OY Vaasa-Umeå A/B (F. E. Nyman, managers), Vaasa, Finland and renamed Örnen.
12.9.1969: Broken up at by Helsingin Romuliike at Helsinki.

Wellamo. [H.J. Reinecke/Ian Farquhar collection]

ILMATAR 1929-1945
2,365g 1,208n 283.1 (oa) (270.1(bp)) x 41.6 x 23.6 feet.
T.3-cyl. by A/S Burmeister & Wain, Copenhagen; 383 NHP. Single screw.
25.5.1929: Completed by A/S Burmeister & Wain, Copenhagen (Yard No. 562) for Finska Ångfartygs A/B.
8.1.1945: Handed over to the USSR as war reparations. Subsequently used as the depot ship EMBA by the Soviet Navy
1963: Deleted from 'Jane's Fighting Ships.'

POLARIS (2) 1933-1945
1,525g 891n 254.1 (oa) (240.9 (bp)) x 34.6 x 15.3 feet.
T.3-cyl. by Stettiner Oderwerke A.G., Stettin; 134 NHP. Single screw.
1954: Two 8-cyl. 4SCSA oil engines by Gôrlitzer Masch., Görlitz.
13.5.1912: Completed by Stettiner Oderwerke A.G., Stettin (Yard No. 632) for the Neue Dampfer-Compagnie A.G., Stettin as PRINZESSIN SOPHIE CHARLOTTE
1922: Renamed PREUSSEN.
1923: Transferred to the Stettiner Dampfer Compagnie A.G., Stettin.
1931: Sold to the 'Renata' Dampfschiffs Gesellschaft Th. Gribel (R.C. Gribel, managers), Stettin.
17.10.1933: Acquired by Finska Ångfartygs A/B and renamed POLARIS, now 1,615g.
19.2.1942: Damaged by fire whilst under repair at Turku.
1945: Handed over to the USSR as war reparations.
1946: Became SESTRORETSK of the Baltic Steamship Company and from 1954 the Murmansk Steamship Company, both part of the Soviet state merchant fleet.
1954: Rebuilt as a motor ship, although 'Lloyd's Register' continued to list her as having her original steam engine.
24.11.1970: Arrived at Split for demolition by Brodospas.
25.1.1972: Work began.

AALLOTAR 1937-1945
2,916g 1,607n 295.4 (oa) x 45.3 x 25.7 feet.
C.4-cyl. Lentz type by Helsingørs Jernskibs- og Maskinbyggeri, Helsingør; 534 NHP. Single screw.
22.5.1937: Completed by Helsingørs Jernskibs- og Maskinbyggeri, Helsingør (Yard No. 242) for Finska Ångfartygs A/B.
28.6.1945: Handed over to the USSR as war reparations to replace ARIADNE and renamed BELOOSTROV for the Baltic Steamship Company, Leningrad.
1956: Transferred to the Black Sea Shipping Company, Odessa.
1968: Transferred to the Sakhalin Shipping Company, Kholmsk.
6.6.1975: Arrived at Iziumiotsu, Japan for demolition by Matsukura Kaiji

ASTREA 1941-1944
3,190g 1,704n 313.2 (oa) x 44.1 x 24.0 feet.
7-cyl. 2SCSA oil engine by Friedrich Krupp Germaniawerft, Kiel; 3,250 BHP. Single screw.
10.1939: Launched by Crichton-Vulkan, Turku (Yard No. 755) for Finska Ångfartygs A/B as ASTREA but laid up after partial completion in 5.1941.
17.2.1944: Sold in a bomb-damaged condition to Stockholms Rederi A/B Svea, Stockholm. It was secretly arranged that she would be sold on to Det Bergenske D/S, Bergen. Rebuilt by A/B Finnboda Varv, Stockholm.
9.1945: Commissioned by Det Bergenske D/S, still with the name ASTREA.
11.1967: Sold to P/f Skipafelagid Føroyar,

Ilmatar. *[Laurence Dunn collection]*

Aallotar. *[Laurence Dunn collection]*

Astrea. *[J. & M. Clarkson]*

Torshavn, Faroes and re-named TJALDUR, surprisingly under the Norwegian flag.
18.7.1969: Engine break down.
28.8.1969: Sold to Metaalhandel en Sloopwereken H.P. Heuvelman NV for breaking.
6.9.1969: Arrived in the Nieuw Waterweg under tow.

FRIDEBORG – A LINK WITH THE TEA CLIPPERS
John Naylon

Richard Marshall Cookson, who died on 10th May 1998 at the age of 89, was one of Britain's most dedicated students of latter-day sail. He enjoyed an international reputation for his encyclopaedic knowledge and painstaking research, and he was unfailingly generous with information - not all of which was acknowledged. He was also an enthusiastic and intrepid photographer, recording not only vessels as they lay moored but also the details of their deck fittings, spars and rigging. Examples of his work can be found in, for instance, the Conway Maritime Press publication 'The Four-Masted Barque *Lawhill*' (Anatomy of the Ship series, 1996). This was a vessel to which he devoted a lifetime's study.

Although Richard Cookson's main interest was the deep-water square-riggers which visited British ports in the interwar years, in his wanderings around the London docks in September 1933 he came across the barquentine *Frideborg* discharging splitwood in the Regent's Canal Dock. In the photographs which illustrate this article he has left us invaluable images of a class of sailing vessel which enjoyed unrivalled fame but which - apart from the *Cutty Sark* - disappeared long ago, for the humble *Frideborg* began life as the tea clipper *Cleta*.

The composite barque *Cleta*
The composite barque *Cleta* was launched in August 1866 - the year of the great tea race from Foochow to London between the *Ariel* and the *Taeping* - by Gardner of Sunderland for John Hay of London; official number 56780, signal flags TPRG. She measured a modest 546 tons gross, 505 tons net, on dimensions 153.3 x 29.5 x 17.2 feet, with a coefficient of under-deck tonnage of 0.63, the same as the *Taeping, Kaisow* and *Black Prince*.

Composite build - a wooden skin on iron frames, beams and floors - seems to have been introduced in India in 1839 when Captain Andrew Henderson built the 450-ton steamer *Assam*. During the 20 years following, there were over thirty applications to the British Patent Office for the use of iron combined with wood for ships' hulls. Rather than a transitional stage between wooden and iron hulls, composite construction should be regarded as a solution to specific difficulties experienced with early iron craft. Though the advantages of iron ships were already recognized by the 1850s and 1860s, when the China tea trade and its clippers were in their prime, tea merchants would not consider iron hulls, believing they impaired the cargo because of condensation in the hold. Moreover, at that time the only known satisfactory anti-fouling for vessels in tropical waters was copper sheathing, but this set up galvanic action when applied to iron hulls. Composite construction was the answer; the builders claiming that it gave all the advantages of an iron hull but none of its disadvantages in the tea trade. The iron frames provided strength to stand up to the pressures of sail carrying and of course were lighter than timber frames of equal strength, so that more cargo could be stowed than in wooden vessels of similar dimensions. Another consideration was the high cost of docking and scraping an iron hull in eastern waters. Composite ships had timber stems, stern posts, keels and planking (although the *Cutty Sark* has iron bulwarks) so that the underwater body could be copper sheathed over tarred felt in the usual way.

A few composite vessels were constructed intermittently in the 1840s and 1850s but the system suddenly became popular among tea clippers about 1863 when the *Taeping* was launched. Lloyd's were suspicious of the system for a while and would at first only give it an 'experimental' classification, subject to survey every two years; however, by 1864 they were sufficiently convinced to give their surveyors instructions to draw up a set of rules, which were issued in 1867.

RICHARD MARSHALL COOKSON 1909-1998

Richard Marshall Cookson was born in the port and mill town of Preston, Lancashire, on 18th February 1909. Denied a sea career - his heart's desire, sparked by a visit to a royal review of shipping on the Mersey at the age of four - by a stern mother and a lack of money for an apprentice's indentures, he indulged his boyhood fantasies by sailing a raft around Preston's Albert Edward Dock, boarding the vessels which called there, and running errands for the foreman of Thomas Ward's shipbreaking yard, where his father worked.

After a grudging apprenticeship to the grocery trade, Cookson spent three years in the Scots Guards at Wellington Barracks, followed by fourteen and a half years in the London Metropolitan Police. It was at this time, in the 1920s and 1930s, that he started his visits to the Australian grain ships and Baltic traders in London and other ports, assiduously building up his research collections and contacts, making numerous friendships among the officers and men of Gustav Erikson's fleet, and becoming a highly-skilled and prize-winning model engineer.

Leaving the police force on medical grounds in 1943, Cookson began a new career as a fitter and turner, steadily improving his engineering skills. In 1956 he emigrated with his family to Rhodesia, working for the Rhodesia Iron and Steel Company and becoming Secretary and President of the Steelworkers' Union of Rhodesia. Ian Smith's Unilateral Declaration of Independence in 1965 prompted a move to Zambia, where for ten years he lectured in engineering at the Northern Technical College in Ndola. On returning to England in 1975, Cookson became superintendent of a block of offices in Chancery Lane, London, next door to the Public Record Office - a happy circumstance which allowed him, among other research, to carry out a three-year study of the official logs of sailing ships 1900-1912.

Throughout a 52-year working life (with never a day's unemployment, as he would proudly say), and in his retirement at Long Sutton, Lincolnshire, and Silverdale, Staffordshire, Richard Cookson collected an immense store of photographs, negatives and written material on nineteenth- and twentieth-century deepwater square riggers. He was a meticulous research worker, constantly checking and correcting his own and others' findings. He achieved global recognition for his specialized knowledge, contributing to authoritative journals and books and maintaining an intense and world-wide correspondence with eminent contemporaries in his field. Although denied his true vocation, Richard Cookson dedicated his life to the ships he loved and he merits respect and gratitude for his important role in preserving their memory.

A number of well-known China clippers were composite built, besides the *Cutty Sark* and *Taeping* (*Ariel, Kaisow, Lahloo, Mofussilite, Norman Court, Sir Lancelot, Thermopylae, Titania, Wild Deer*) as well as emigrant and wool clippers such as the *Sobraon* and *Torrens*. Another composite vessel was engaged in the interwar splitwood trade along with the *Frideborg/Cleta:* the barque *Sverre* (ex-*Sigurd*), built in 1872 as the steamer *Aalto* and converted to sail in 1920; she was the last composite-built ship to carry cargo. The only remaining examples of the system are the *Cutty Sark* at Greenwich and the *Carrick*, whose fate currently lies in the balance in Scotland. The *Carrick* was built in 1864 by Pile of Sunderland as the 791-ton *City of Adelaide* for Devitt and Moore's emigrant trade to Australia; for many years she served as an RNVR club ship at Glasgow.

Although adopted by the Admiralty, composite construction had a relatively short life, curtailed by advances in iron and steel building; after the 1870s it was used only in isolated instances in the Royal Navy and in private yachts. Nevertheless, it was a successful and durable system. Composite vessels were strongly built and sometimes had remarkably long lives, outlasting their iron and steel sisters - witness the career of the *Cleta*.

Tea clipper days

The *Cleta* had no pretensions to rivalling the crack clippers and seems to have attracted little notice in her tea-carrying days of 1867-73. She does not merit a mention in Captain Andrew Shewan's lengthy reminiscences in the old series of 'Sea Breezes' or in Lubbock's 'China Clippers', possibly because she traded exclusively from China and Japan to New York.

David MacGregor lists the *Cleta's* tea passages as follows: season 1867-8 Hong Kong-New York 127 days; 1868-9 Foochow-New York 104 days (the best passage of

the season); 1870-1 Canton-New York 114 days; 1871-2 Shanghai-New York not known; 1872-3 (her last tea passage) Yokohama-New York 122 days. The *Cleta* was commanded throughout by Captain Middleton. For purposes of comparison, among the fastest passages from China to New York were those of the *Sea Witch* (Hong Kong-New York 74½ days in 1849 and Canton-New York 77 days in 1847-8) and the *Swordfish* (Shanghai-New York 81 days in 1859-60).

While owned in London the *Cleta* made most of her outward passages to China from Liverpool, which is a reminder that while London shipowners dominated the tea trade, Liverpool also sent out some notable vessels. James Beazley owned the *Robin Hood, Friar Tuck, Jessie Beazley* and *Vision;* Brocklebanks the *Scawfell, Whinfell, Burdwan, Everest* and *Maiden Queen;* and Taylor, Potter and Co. had the *Chrysolite*, commanded by the renowned Anthony Enright.

In the colonial trade

By 1873 the tea trade under sail was effectively finished, due to the opening of the Suez Canal in 1869, and the *Cleta* was sold by Hay to Balfour, Williamson and Co., Liverpool, who put her into the Australian trade. Curiously, although while she was London-owned she had traded to China mainly from Liverpool, now that she was Liverpool-owned she sailed mainly from London. She spent 10 years sailing to Australia, then in 1884 went to California and in 1885 to Valparaiso. On her return from Chile she was sold to J.S. Davis, also of Liverpool, but spent most of 1886-7 laid up in Princes Dock.

Sold to Scandinavia

Davis only kept her for two years, selling her in 1887 to E.T. Norrman of Malmö, Sweden. Given the homely name of *Nelly & Mathilda*, she now embarked upon a remarkable

September 1933: the *Frideborg* lies in Regent's Canal Dock, London, the traditional venue for ice and timber droghers, discharging splitwood into lighters. She had arrived at Gravesend on 30th August, 20 days from Sundsvall, and would leave Gravesend on 24th September for Uleåborg. The standing rigging of the fore and mizzen masts is set up by deadeyes and lanyards, indicating that these are the original spars, whereas that of the mainmast, dating from the 1917 re-rigging as a barquentine, is set up by bottle screws. The fore royal yard has been sent down for economy's sake. One is struck by the small size of the vessel, to undertake almost 20 years of voyaging to China, New York, Australia, California and Chile.

career of 50 years of Baltic timber droghing, marred only by collisions in 1893, 1900 and 1907, in which year she also stranded. By 1907 she had passed to E. Jansson, also of Malmö. In 1916 Jansson sold her via Olsson, Johansson and Friberg to Björknäs Aktieb. (G. Erstad, manager) of Björknäs, Sweden, who in 1917 substantially rebuilt her and re-rigged her as a barquentine. Wartime freights were evidently still obtaining, making it worthwhile to spend money on such an elderly vessel. Indeed, in 1919 she made an excursion out of home waters to Lisbon, for a very profitable cargo of 250 tons of cork bark and 520 tons of case goods. The good times soon ended, however: in 1923 Björknäs Aktieb. went out of business. At the end of 1926 the liquidators sold the *Nelly & Mathilda* to J.O. Halmström of Ramsjöstrand, who in 1926 sent her under the Finnish flag. Bought initially by V.A. Engblom, Eliel Henriksson and F. Henriksson of Kumlinge in the Åland Islands, in 1927 she ended up completely in the hands of Eliel Henriksson, who renamed her *Frideborg* and registered her in Mariehamn.

In the splitwood trade
Under the Finnish flag the *Frideborg* found humble but useful employment for a further ten years, bringing pit props and small timber from the sawmills in the Gulfs of Bothnia and Finland to Sweden, Denmark, Germany, London, Grangemouth, Grimsby and Yarmouth. Sometimes the old clipper could still show a turn of speed. In 1933 she went from Sundsvall to Grimsby in 12 days; in 1935 from London to Kemi in 23 days, Kemi to Yarmouth in 24 days and Yarmouth to Hamina in 13 days; and in 1936 from Piteå to Yarmouth in 26 days on two occasions, and from Yarmouth to Piteå in 22 days.

The end of a long career
In 1937, still as staunch as ever, the *Frideborg* made a good passage of 25 days from Kalix, at the very head of the Gulf of Bothnia, to Gravesend, but on her return trip went ashore at Holmögadd near Kalix on 7th September. She was got off without even leaking, thanks to her sound construction, and was sailed into Luleå and laid up over the winter; but her owner declined to have her repaired and so, at the age of 71 years, she was condemned and broken up. In 1977 her entire poop accommodation was reported as still in use as a summerhouse near Luleå. The *Cleta/Nelly & Mathilda/Frideborg* had been continuously engaged in trade from 1866 to 1937, making her the last of the China tea fleet afloat, apart from the *Cutty Sark,* and the last tea clipper to earn a living at sea.

The photographs
Richard Cookson's pictures provide a valuable record of the construction, arrangements and fittings of a tea clipper of the 1860s. They enable us to compare the simple build of a second-class clipper with the superior appointments of a first-class vessel like the *Cutty Sark;* even allowing for the fact that the *Cleta* must have received many hard knocks in her 71 years' career, her fabric appears modest, even humble. And they give us a glimpse of the homely and anachronistic conditions of Baltic seafaring under sail in the 1930s.

A closer view of the starboard bow shows some more intimate details, including the crew's scanty washing hung up to dry, and the closet at the break of the anchor deck, flushed by hand with a can. The navigation lights (the lamps have been removed as a precaution against theft) are secured to the lanyards of the fore shrouds. Abaft the deckhouse a small engine house stands at the foot of the mainmast. Small timber-loading ports have been cut into the hull. The planking of the bulwarks is characteristically thinner, forming a step with the top of the planksheer. The old method of getting the anchors on board is visible. The fish-tackle pendant is secured to the fore topmast hounds. The hook on the lower block of the tackle (triced to the foot of the forestay when not in use) would be hooked to a fluke of the anchor by a man going overside. The anchor might then be brought up close to the cathead and held there by the cat fall (the chain hanging below the cathead) or hoisted on board. Beyond the *Frideborg* lies a three-masted bald-headed auxiliary schooner, North American-built to judge by the poop and forecastle.

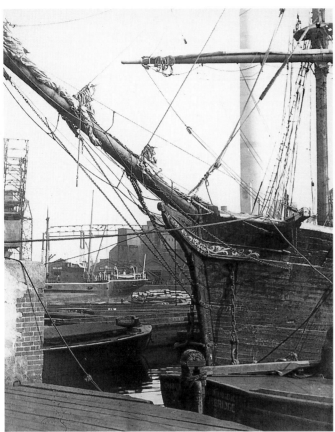

Above left: Very little of the classic clipper bow here: the rabbet line runs straight from the forefoot to the knightheads. The bow decoration is modest: no figurehead - just a fiddle head and simple trail boards. The spike bowsprit is not original, of course, but a consequence of the vessel's collision in 1907 with the barque *Bonden* of Grimstad; the *Cleta* would originally have carried a bowsprit and jibboom, as evidenced by the bobstay plate in the lower part of the stem. The cat stopper chain, used to suspend the anchor below the cathead, hangs in a loop.

Above right: Rather than a forecastle head the *Frideborg/Cleta* has just a small anchor deck, barely three feet high, under which could be kept stores and livestock. It is shaped around the windlass so that the crew can stand on the anchor deck to work the windlass levers. The anchor deck is level with the main rail and there are no guard rails - just a tapered spirketting running from the bow to the break of the anchor deck. The capstan looks like a modern addition, just used for warping; a double-geared capstan such as this, with two rims of holes, would ordinarily suggest a patent mechanical

winch below, which the *Frideborg/Cleta* did not carry. A simple pin rail takes the head sheets. The inboard ends of the catheads are bolted through the deck to a heavy catbeam on the underside and seem to be further secured by chain lashings. The catheads carry the cat stopper chains, part of the anchor-releasing gear, and eye bolts through which would originally have passed iron whisker booms to take the jibboom guys. Also visible on the anchor deck are a crowbar for prising loose the turns of the anchor chains and, to port, a fish hook for bringing the flukes of the anchor up close to the rail.

Right: 'Armstrong's patent'. By the mid-nineteenth century the horizontal barrel windlass was the standard device for raising anchors in wooden sailing vessels and, despite its slow and back-breaking method of operation, remained in use to the very end of commercial sail. The octagonal barrel of oak or hardwood is faced with iron whelps to grip the cable when heaving in. The barrel is supported on two greenheart timbers - the carrick bitts - extending to the deck below and supported on the forward side by knees to resist the pull of the anchors and chains. Another large greenheart post, the pawl bitt, is situated forward of the barrel on the centre line and is carried down to the 'tween deck beams or even to the keelson. It carries a pawl which engages a ratchet wheel on the barrel to prevent the windlass reversing and the cable running out. The pawl bitt also takes the heel tenon of the bowsprit.

Outside the carrick bitts are small wooden warping drums, originally pierced with square holes into which handspikes were inserted to heave the windlass round. From about 1832 onwards the handspikes were replaced by the pump-handle arrangement ('You up, me down') seen in the picture. A pivoted crosshead is fitted on top of the pawl bitt, into which fit two hand levers, eight feet long and terminating in horns through which ash rods are inserted so that more than one man can operate each lever. Vertical purchase rods from the crosshead carry ratchets which rotate the windlass drums on the upward movement by engaging in the toothed purchase wheels seen on each side of the pawl wheel.

The curved greenheart strongback connecting the carrick bitts and pawl bitt is used for tricing up the chain cable, as here on the port cable. A bracket carrying the ship's bell passes through the strongback, with a metal spike stuck through a shackle for striking the bell. The anchor chain takes its customary three

turns over and under the windlass barrel and is here piled in a heap to be clear of the splitwood deckload. Ordinarily at sea it would be ranged along the deck, taken aft and led through the spurling pipes into the chain locker, an iron tank situated on the keelson at the foot of the foremast, divided in two for the port and starboard cables.

Though slow to operate - it could take an hour to get in 10-11 fathoms of cable - the whole construction was extremely strong since it was an integral part of the vessel's bow and not simply bolted to the deck. Abaft the windlass is another classic item of sailing-ship deck equipment - the dolly winch, used for lighter work.

Right: Looking forward from the port quarterdeck. The cabin trunk, with the mizzen mast rising through it, has a properly laid deck with guard rails and is used for conning the ship. The coved sides were commonly covered with painted canvas. The saloon stove pipe projects through the roof alongside the skylight.

Below left: The after-deck arrangements of the *Cleta* were similar to those of a number of other tea clippers, including the *Falcon* and *Pak Wan*. Cabins and saloon are located in an 'Aberdeen house' on the main deck, with a raised quarterdeck on three sides level with the rail. The house is entered by a door on the main deck and a companion at the after end. The forward end of the coach roof is dished to allow water to run

off. There is no elaborate panelling, not even at the front of the house - just tongue-and-groove boarding.

The low wings of the raised quarterdeck provide room for sails and stores, with removable panels behind the portable steps. In the foreground, between the fore and main masts, we have a rare view of the classic Scandinavian timber drogher's windmill pump and a pile of stout posts which have been used to secure the *Frideborg's* deck load. A representative selection of her cargo lies in the lighters alongside. She carries two typical Scandinavian prams, one on the cabin roof and another alongside the starboard rail.

Note the small size of the main and after hatches.

Looking forward from the port quarterdeck. The cabin trunk, with the mizzen mast rising through it, has a properly laid deck with guard rails and is used for conning the ship. The coved sides were commonly covered with painted canvas. The saloon stove pipe projects through the roof alongside the skylight.

Below right: Another view of the windmill pump, with three members of the crew enjoying a break - one in his going-ashore clothes. Even after almost 70 years of service, the *Frideborg's* hull was still tight and apparently the pump was little used.

The windmill is supported on two standards placed up against the after end of the deckhouse. There are four arms and the sails can be 'reefed' or pleated when not needed. A rod and crank connect the sails to the pump and there is a bar for turning the apparatus to catch the wind. The massive sheet anchor lies close up against the small engine house. The deckhouse also is a modest tongue-and-groove affair. The galley chimney sticks up among the raffle of timber baulks, towing hawser and boat, which has been lifted off the skids. The purpose of the battens on the main mast (also fitted on the mizzen) is not known.

Above: A starboard-side view of the donkey engine (a later addition), windmill pump and deckhouse. The engine house may originally have been the galley. Shoes well polished, the shore-goer sits on an upturned pram.

Right: The entire fore mast - top, crosstrees and spars - appears to be original and is typical of the period.

SOURCES AND ACKNOWLEDGEMENTS

We thank all who gave permission for their photographs to be used, and for help in finding photographs we are particularly grateful to Tony Smith, Jim McFaul and David Whiteside of the World Ship Photo Library; to Ian Farquhar, F.W. Hawks, Bill Laxon, Peter Newall, Ivor Rooke, William Schell, George Scott; and to David Hodge and Bob Todd of the National Maritime Museum, and other museums and institutions listed.

Research sources have included the *Registers* of William Schell and Tony Starke, *Lloyd's Register, Lloyd's Confidential Index, Lloyd's War Losses, Mercantile Navy Lists, Marine News* and *Shipbuilding and Shipping Record*. Use of the facilities of the World Ship Society's Central Record, the Guildhall Library, the National Archives and Lloyd's Register of Shipping are gratefully acknowledged. Particular thanks also to Heather Fenton for editorial and indexing work, and Marion Clarkson for accountancy services.

Migrants and butter
Thanks to Leena Scutt, Laurence Dunn and Ambrose Greenway for their help with this article. Sources include *Lloyd's Registers; Lloyd's Confidential Indexes; The Scandinavian Shipping Gazette*, Thure Malmberg and Arnold Neumann *The White Ships*, Finland Line, Helsinki, 1971; Matti Pietikäinen and Bengt Sjöström *The Ships of our First Century: The EFFOA Fleet 1883-1983*, EFFOA, Helsinki, 1983.

Frideborg - a link with the tea clippers
A lengthy description of the *Frideborg's* career is given by Lars Grönstrand in his *Åländska skeppsporträtt i ord och bild*, Mariehamn, 1978, pp.87-96. Composite construction is discussed in David R. MacGregor, *Fast Sailing Ships 1775-1875: Their Design and Construction*, Nautical Publishing Co. Ltd., Lymington, Hampshire, 1973, pp.156-62. Passing mention of the *Cleta* can be found in the same author's *The Tea Clippers: Their History and Development 1833-1875*, Conway Maritime Press, 2nd edition, 1983. Deck fittings and layouts are described in Harold A. Underhill, *Deep-Water Sail*, Brown, Son and Ferguson, Ltd., Glasgow, 1952 and in George F. Campbell, *China Tea Clippers*, Adlard Coles, London, 1974. For the pleasures of old-time windlass and anchor work, see G.L. Harvey in *Sea Breezes* (Old Series), Vol.19, No.189, September, 1935, p.280; Captain John W. Davies, 'The old-fashioned windlass: some more interesting reflections', *idem.*, Vol.20, No.191, October, 1935, pp.10-12; and Douglas Bennet, *Schooner Sunset: The Last British Sailing Coasters*, Chatham Publishing, London, 2001, pp.61-8.

Bosphorus ferries
Special thanks to Jochen Kruesmann for providing histories of the vessels and for patiently responding to our questions. Sources include: Alistair Deayton, 'The Bosphorus and Beyond', *Sea Breezes* (March, April, May) 1988; Alistair Deayton, *Steamships of Europe*, Conway Maritime Press Ltd., London 1988; Christopher Austin, 'Istanbul's Clyde-built Ferries', *Ships Monthly*, December 1995.

SARAYBURNU (opposite)
Fairfield Shipbuilding and Engineering Co. Ltd., Glasgow; 1910, 434gt, 154 feet
Two T 3-cyl. by the builder
With the stokers hard at work, *Sarayburnu* lays a fine pall of smoke over the Bosphorus as she makes her approach to Ortaköy on a morning service to the city's main terminal in May 1979. Built for Şirket-i Hayriye, her subsequent name and ownership changes were typical of those of several similar ferries built for that company over the next 30 years.

In her original guise she carried both a number and name: *No. 65 - Sarayburnu,* but in 1944 when Şirket-i Hayriye was taken into public ownership, all their vessels were given uniform *Bosphorus* names which now prefixed the individual vessel's number. Thus as *Bosphorus No. 65* she came under the auspices of Türkiye Cümhuriyeti Münakalât Vekâleti Devlet Denizyollari ve Limanari İşletme Umum Müdürlügü (Republic of Turkey, Ministry of Communications - General Direction for the Exploitation of the State Lines). In 1952 the state enterprise was reformed into the better known, and infinitely more recognisable, Denizcillik Bankasi T.A.O. - often referred to as the Turkish Bank Line, in which the ferries were managed by the City Lines Administration (Şehir Hatlari İşletmesi). The *Bosphorus* ferries then reverted to their original names but, although the operating number continued to be displayed on boards mounted on the bridge wings, this was not now included as part of the registered name.* Following *Sarayburnu's* withdrawal in 1984 she was sold and converted into a restaurant cruise-ship, with her twin reciprocating engines replaced by diesels. Her new career was brought to an abrupt end in 1993 when she was wrecked after terrorists set off explosive charges on board. *[Paul Boot]*

* For all other Şirket-i Hayriye ships this number is shown in brackets following the name in the caption header.

Bosphorus Ferries

BOĞAZIÇI (66) (above)
Fairfield Co. Ltd., Glasgow; 1910, 434gt, 153 feet
Two T 3-cyl. by the builder
Delivered just a few weeks after her sister *Sarayburnu*, *Boğaziçi* makes a splendid sight as she announces her arrival at Üsküdar on the Asian side of the Bosphorus. The board bearing her operating number is prominent, as is the searchlight near the bow with its canvas shelter for the operator. After being taken out of service in 1982, she too became a restaurant cruise-ship and was also to suffer a catastrophic fate; in this instance run down by a Russian vessel in 1992 whilst at anchor off Emirgân.
[*Paul Boot*]

Bosphorus Ferries

Paul Boot

Steam ferries have operated on the Bosphorus for more than a century and a half, providing a unique commuter service between two continents. For the last sixty years the fleet has formed part of the state controlled shipping concern, now known as the Turkish Maritime Administration, in which the Istanbul ferries are operated by the City Lines Administration. A campaign to clean up the city in the 1980s brought an end to the days of the coal fired steamers, the oldest of which had been built before the First World War. Amazingly, four survivors of a class of nine compound-engined ferries built by Fairfields over forty years ago remain in service.

KALENDAR (67) (opposite page bottom) and **GÜZELHISAR** (68) (below)
both: Hawthorn, Leslie and Co. Ltd., Newcastle-upon-Tyne; 1911, 453gt, 152 feet
Two T 3-cyl. by Wallsend Slipway Co. Ltd., Wallsend
A considerable number of ferries were built for Sirket-i-Hayriye in the early years of the last century and these two from Hawthorn Leslie were very similar to the preceding Fairfield built sisters.

Kalendar was withdrawn in 1984 and sold for use as a training ship. *Güzelhisar* remained in service until December 1986, by then the last of the coal-fired veterans. Five years later, some preparatory work was done to rebuild her as a museum ship, but the stripped down hull has since languished at Tuzla. *[both Nigel Jones]*

ERENKÖY (above)
Soc. de Ateliers et Chantiers de France, Dunkerque; 1911, 567gt, 155 feet.
Two T 3-cyl. by the builder
No. 70 - *Ziya* was one of a pair of slightly larger sister ships ordered from this French yard by Sirket-i Hayriye and was renamed *Erenköy* in 1933 when she passed to AKAY Idaresi, part of the Turkish state shipping company, and later to Sehir Hatlari. After withdrawal in 1983, she was sold for conversion to yet another restaurant cruise-ship but, unlike her unlucky counterparts, she is reportedly still in service. Seen here passing Arnavutköy in May 1979, such impressive smoke emissions would find little favour with the city's authorities a few years later. *[Paul Boot]*

BURGAZ

Soc. Anon. des Chantiers et Ateliers de Provence, Port de Bouc; 1912, 697gt, 201 feet
Two T 3-cyl. by Soc. Anon. des Chantiers et Ateliers de Provence, Marseilles

Prior to the full nationalisation of the ferry fleets in 1944, the Turkish state shipping company had for many years operated its own ferries under a complex succession of ownership titles. With its Bosphorus operations extending to Adalar, the Princes' Islands, in the Sea of Marmara, the raised forecastle head on *Burgaz* was a desirable feature and this hull configuration was adopted for all the later passenger ferries subsequently built by Şehir Hatlari İşletmesi.

Apart from conversion to oil burning in 1961, *Burgaz,* like most of the ferries, remained little changed during her lengthy career. Her apparently less obvious exhaust emissions gained her an extra year or two and she was not withdrawn until 1988 and subsequently reduced to a floating pontoon.

[Roy Fenton]

HALAS (71) (left and below)

Fairfield Co. Ltd., Glasgow; 1915, 584gt, 153 feet
Two T 3-cyl. by the builder

In 1913 Şirket-i Hayriye placed orders for three further ferries with British yards but the outbreak of war the following year resulted in only one being built. This was taken over by the Royal Navy during construction and, named *Waterwitch,* she was used as a despatch vessel. It was not until 1921 that she was released by the Navy and finally acquired by her rightful owners. On a totally still evening 58 years later, *Halas* (below) lays a perfect smoke trail down the Bosphorus, providing another reason why the days of the coal burners would not be lasting much longer. *Halas* was laid up in 1983 and sold three years after to become yet another vehicle for marine catering. The conversion was to be a sympathetic one however as this 1995 view of her in Göcek Bay, near Fethiye, shows (left). [Paul Boot; Nigel Bowker]

SUVAT (above)
Atlas Werke .A.G., Bremen; 1938, 923gt, 205 feet
Two T 3-cyl. by Christiansen & Meyer, Hamburg
The ferry fleet of the Turkish state shipping company underwent no fewer than four of its many reorganisations during the 1930s, during which two new ships were ordered and delivered. These were of a very similar design to the *Heybeliada*, built ten years previously, and the much older *Burgaz*. *Suvat*, and her sister *Ulev*, both underwent a reconstruction in 1965 when they were given a profile very similar to the 1961 Fairfield-built class and were converted to oil burning at the same time. *Suvat* was withdrawn in 1988 and eight years later work began to rebuild her as a floating restaurant, but this has yet to be completed. In August 1980, *Suvat* passes the Blue Mosque and Aya Sofya on her way into Istanbul. *[Jim McFaul]*

KOCATAŞ (75) (right) and **SARİYER (76)** (below)
Sirket-i Hayriye, Istanbul-Hasköy; 1937 and 1938, 157gt, 108 feet
T 3-cyl. by MacTaggart, Scott and Co. Ltd., Leith
Around the same time, Şirket-i Hayriye built two smaller single-screw steamers at their own yard using engines and boilers dating from 1913 which are presumed to have been recovered from other ships. With long, enclosed upper saloon decks, these two ferries were not the most elegant members of their fleet, particularly when seen bow-on as in this view of *Kocatas* (right) at Bebek. They were withdrawn in 1984 and 1983 respectively. *Sariyer,* seen laying off at Beykoz in 1979 (below), was extensively rebuilt as a motorship and renamed *Paradise* in 1986 for her new role in the floating restaurant business. *[Paul Boot]*

ANADOLUHİSARI (above)
N.V. Werf "Gusto", Schiedam;, 1949, 561gt, 179 feet
Two T 3-cyl. by L. Smit & Zoon, Kinderdijk
The first new ships to be ordered by Şehir Hatlari İşletmesi after nationalisation came from a consortium of three Dutch shipyards; each building two of a total of six twin-screw steamers that had a very similar profile to the ferries of the earlier state-owned fleet, but were somewhat smaller.

With a commendably clear exhaust, *Anadoluhisari* steams past Arnavutköy on her way up the Bosphorus in April 1981, five years before she was withdrawn. *[Nigel Jones]*

YALOVA (below)
Verschure & Co.'s Scheepswerf en Machinewerk, Amsterdam; 1948, 561gt, 179 feet
Two T 3-cyl. by builder
Yalova was the first of the Dutch-built sextet to be delivered and the last to be withdrawn, remaining in service until 1995. She is seen here arriving at the Eminönü terminal in October 1988 when she was already the only one of her peers still operational. Behind her, Galata Bridge spans the entrance to the Golden Horn with work in progress on piling the foundations for the new bridge. To the right, the fourteeenth century Galata Tower presides over Istanbul's waterfront. *[Nigel Jones]*

KUZGUNÇUK (above)
Fairfield Shipbuilding and Engineering Co. Ltd., Glasgow; 1961, 781gt, 229 feet
Four C 2-cyl. by builder
The Dutch vessels were the last coal burners to be built and for the next decade all new passenger ferries were motorships. Towards the end of 1959, however, in a surprising move that is almost certainly without parallel, no fewer than nine, double-compound-engined steamers were ordered from Fairfields, all of which were delivered during 1961. *Kuzguncuk* was one of the first pair to be constructed, being launched the same day as her sister *Kanlica* on 21st December 1960 and delivered three months later. This broadside view of her illuminated by the late afternoon sunshine in October 1988 shows the fine lines of this class to advantage. She was taken out of service in 1999 and broken up at Aliaga in April 2000. *[Nigel Jones]*

PENDIK (below)
Fairfield Shipbuilding and Engineering Co. Ltd., Glasgow; 1961, 781gt, 229 feet
Four C 2-cyl. by L. Christiansen & Meyer, Hamburg
Of the nine vessels, six had their compound engines manufactured by Fairfield under licence, whilst *Pendik* was one of the three whose engines were constructed in Germany. Each of the two propellors is driven by a pair of the compounds connected directly to the shaft. The main auxiliaries - generators and pumps, as well as the steering gear - are all steam-powered too, supplied from two single-ended, oil-fired Scotch boilers.

With passengers crowding the gangway positions, *Pendik* rounds up prior to berthing at Eminönü in September 1989. Three years later she was gutted by fire after a terrorist attack and was scrapped in 1993. *[Nigel Bowker]*

The four Fairfield steamers that have been retained - all of which share the same principal details as *Kuzgunçuk* and which are therefore not repeated - owe their survival largely to their substantial passenger capacity. Their certificate for nearly 2,000 persons is put to good use during the peak time services and sometimes on the longer trips to Adalar in summer months. Despite the construction of two bridges over the Bosphorus, the ferries still remain an important means of transport for many. On a very fresh October morning in 1988, *Kanlica* steams west, with the older of the two suspension bridges straddling the skyline (above). In the distance, another Turkish veteran, the cargo-passenger liner *Akdeniz* (8,809/1955), can be seen berthed at Ortaköy.

[Nigel Jones]

The surviving quartet includes the last two members of the class to be built, *İhsan Kalmaz* and *Turan Emeksiv*, both of which were launched on 3rd July 1961. *İhsan Kalmaz* commemorated the lieutenant killed in the military uprising against the Turkish prime minister Adnan Menderes the previous year and in 1983 the lieutenant was given his full military title when the ship was renamed *Tegmen Ali İhsan Kalmaz*. The vessels have obviously been well maintained as this view of *Tegmen Ali İhsan Kalmaz* leaving Karaköy in June 2003 shows (left). [Nigel Jones]

All of the class remain largely as originally built and the only external modification has been the enclosure of the formerly open central section of the bridge between the two conning positions at the wings. It is particularly pleasing to note that the Turkish line has not felt the need to bring in a firm of image consultants to give it a new identity and has retained its traditional orange, white and black funnel colours carrying the star, crescent and crossed anchors insignia. In May 1979, *Turan Emeksiv* gets under way for the short crossing to Haydarpaşa and Kadiköy (right). [Paul Boot]

A living museum; a shiplover's delight; a wonderful tourist attraction. The steam ferries are all of these but above all they were, and still are, an essential means of transport for many people. These three views show some aspects of their day to day life.

Above: *Heybeliada* (699/1928) at Istanbul's Karaköy pier in 1971 with a least eight other ferries to be seen including *İhsan Kalmaz* (781/1961) arriving to the left.

Right: market day at Emirgân as passengers disembark from *Haydarpaşa* with their wares.

Below: a very well loaded *Büyükdere* (561/1948) leaves Bebek on an evening commuter run to Sariyer in 1979. Crowded - yes, but a world apart from the delayed 17.15 to Milton Keynes! [*top Jim McFaul collection; middle and lower Paul Boot*)

WAVECREST FOLLOW UP

The feature on the *Wavecrest* and her running mate *Tidecrest* in *Record* 27 prompted Paul Boot and Dave Salisbury to loan us photographs of another interesting member of the British-flag Ivanovic fleet, the *Skycrest* (9,455/1962). She too was built by Societé des Forges et Chantiers de la Mediterranée but - with all superstructure aft - had a totally different profile to *Wavecrest* and *Tidecrest,* as if her owners were exploring every combination of accommodation, bridge and engine position. In common with the other two, however, she had heavy-lift equipment on her foremast.

Skycrest was built for Crest Shipping Co. Ltd., but was quickly transferred to another Ivanovic company, Cove Shipping Co. Ltd., both being registered in Nassau. In 1968 Ivanovics received an offer for her from West Hartlepool Steam Navigation Co. Ltd. and she became their *Grantleyhall.* Like *Wavecrest,* she had been built with an eye to charter to liner companies, and Paul Boot photographed her on 7th October 1972 in Harrison colours in the West Float at Birkenhead (top). The almost inevitable move to Greek ownership came in 1976, when sold to L.M. Valmas and Son, and renamed *Areti S.* Valmas' ships were operated by Syros Shipping Co. Ltd., and she is seen in their colourful and attractive funnel colours in Dave

Salisbury's photograph in the Nieuw Waterweg in July 1981 (middle).

Areti S was laid up at Piraeus in July 1983, but in 1984 was reactivated and - surprisingly - put back into British registration as *Eurco Wizard.* This may have been a temporary registration, whilst awaiting a survey, as within a few months she had been sold to Chinese breakers, although demolition did not begin until mid-1985. Thanks also to Dennis Cook for alerting us to *Skycrest.*

The *Wavecrest* feature speculated about two possible sisters, and A.D. Frost tells us that, in fact, she had only one. Built in 1957 by the same yard she was not heavily geared and named *Astwi,* owned by K/S Harwi (Rolf Wigands Rederi),

Bergen. She was renamed *Tai Shou* after being sold in 1966 to Taiwan Navigation Co. Ltd., Keelung and was scrapped at Kaohsiung in 1981. Several similar ships were built but were slightly larger and were classified as bulk carriers.

To complete the story of *Wavecrest,* Dave Salisbury also supplied a slide of her as *John Leo,* a name she carried from 1978 to 1982 when owned by Golden Continent Shipping Co. Ltd. She is seen in the Bosphorus during June 1981 (bottom).

Paul Boot points out that *Wavecrest* was built around two years after the first of the Stülcken-fitted 'Hansa' ships, and could not be a forerunner of these heavy-lift ships as the article suggested.

THE CUNARD REEFERS
Stephen Howells

With their fleets of conventional cargo liners replaced by a handful of container vessels, British liner companies had to diversify in the 1970s if they wanted to make use of their well-trained crews and ship operating experience. In 1972 Cunard began to take delivery of eight Spanish-built bulk carriers which were painted in the colours of its Brocklebank subsidiary, albeit with uninspired *Cunard* —- names. Later in the decade, mindful of the refrigerated ships operated by another subsidiary, Port Line, Cunard was tempted into the reefer market. To appreciate the nature of the temptation, it is necessary to look back a few years.

The Maritime Fruit Carriers debacle

In the early 1970s Maritime Fruit Carriers, an Israeli-US consortium, had negotiated a deal with the Swan Hunter Group in which vessels ordered from the shipbuilder would be financed by Swan Maritime, 75% owned by Maritime Fruit Carriers and 25% by Swan Hunter. The concept of builders helping to finance ships was by no means new; it had been common practice in the nineteenth century for shipyards to take shares in ships or

to provide mortgages in order to obtain orders. However, when announced in February 1973, the Maritime Fruit Carriers deal was a major one, accounting for no less than 35% of the UK shipbuilding order book in 1975. It involved reefers built by Smith's Dock, which had been a Swan Hunter subsidiary since 1966. But the real prize was the order for up to 26 vessels including 110,000 deadweight ore-oil carriers and 250,000 deadweight tankers to be built for Swan Maritime on the Tyne. These were Swan Maritime's undoing. The tanker market collapsed in 1975 and early in the following year it was disclosed that Maritime Fruit Carriers could not pay bank debts of $12 million, and owed another $7.5 million to suppliers. The failure of Maritime Fruit Carriers forced Swan Hunter to its knees, the shipbuilder being saved only by intervention from the British Government, who at that time were concerned with keeping shipyards open to build naval craft. This paved the way for nationalisation of the British shipbuilding industry; indeed, so dire was their financial position that Swans were said to be grateful to be bought by the state.

The four Smith's Dock-built reefers were built to a design originating at the Drammen yard, and were originally given 'Clipper' names by Maritime Fruit Carriers. Left is seen *Edinburgh Clipper* in 1975, her hull already rust-streaked. Below she is seen as *Alsatia* on the Nieuw Waterweg in August 1979. The four As carried Salen colours throughout their relatively brief Cunard careers.
[Jim McFaul collection; David Salisbury]

Cunard tempted

Maritime Fruit Carriers had a massive fleet of reefers, 42 at its peak, and these coming on the market clearly depressed the price. Cunard could not resist them. It undoubtedly seemed an opportunity to get into a growing market and a more prestigious one than that for bulk carriers, which were no more than the modern equivalent of the tramp, and subject to cut-throat competition. That the reefers were already British flagged, avoiding the expense of any surveys and modifications need for UK registry, was another attraction. It is worth quoting at length from a letter about the deal which Nigel Broackes, Chairman of Cunard's then owner Trafalgar House Investments Ltd., wrote to his shareholders in December 1976.

'We believe that there have been no fundamental design improvements which make these vessels less attractive than new ships, which would cost substantially more than the price we have paid.

Refrigerated cargo ships of this type carry mainly perishable foodstuffs on a world-wide basis, according to

seasonal requirements, and there would appear to be an increasing demand for this form of transportation. The banana trade continues throughout the year, whereas the citrus fruit season runs from December to July. Deciduous fruit is moved from March to July and the ships also carry fish, meat and dairy produce. The Fleet is highly automated and economic in terms of labour. The vessels are fast, being the modern equivalent of the Clippers after which the UK built vessels were named by Maritime. Their names have now been changed to ones used by previous Cunard ships.

To be a relevant force in the trade a shipowner needs to be able to make successive voyages throughout a season and to have back-up vessels available. We regard ten vessels as constituting a small but adequate unit to make a substantial entry into the trade. The vessels, with their sophisticated multi-purpose refrigeration and cargo-handling equipment, are expensive and relatively slow to build: additions to world capacity over the next two or three years will be very few. Charter hire in the trade is customarily paid in US dollars. The Fleet will operate internationally and we have matched our borrowings to the dollar income we will receive.'

The Salen connection

Broackes continued 'Maritime and Salenrederierna SA (Salen) of Stockholm had since 1972 pooled their interests in this field in which they together constituted the largest independent group in the world: the present purchase will give us an opportunity to become a significant force in the field, operating under the UK flag. We hope to enter into a long term association with Salen and initially we have signed charters with them in respect of each of the vessels for a period of two years. Salen,

The two Oslo-built, intermediate-sized reefers bought by Cunard were given names beginning C. *Cantaloup* seen in the uppermost view during March 1974 was to become *Carinthia*. Her sister *Orange* became *Carmania*, seen middle in Canada Dock, Liverpool during April 1979. On sale by Cunard, she was renamed *Perseus* by Kappa Maritime, seen bottom on the Nieuw Waterweg in August 1989. *[World Ship Photo Library 40952; Jim McFaul collection; David Salisbury]*

who have operated these vessels in the past for Maritime, have taken delivery from us; initially the four smaller Clipper class vessels will continue to be managed by Whitco Limited, a UK subsidiary of the Salen group, but in due course we will manage all ten vessels, thus providing continuing employment for British seamen.'

According to Broackes, it was originally envisaged that Cunard would buy 13 reefers, but in the event 12 were purchased of which two were sold on to W. Bruns of Hamburg. The Norwegian-built *Maranga* became *Brunsland* (9,742/1972) and the *London Clipper* eventually became *Salinas* (6,676/1972). As an aside, two others of the Clipper class were bought by Blue Star, the British-built *Newcastle Clipper* becoming *Trojan Star* (6.680/1973) and her Drammen-built sister *Labrador Clipper* becoming *Tuscan Star* (6,671/1972).

The price to Cunard was around $86 million; some $50 million coming from British and US banks, and $9 million from the original, British government-backed finance of the building costs. Trafalgar House provided the remaining $27 million. Broackes noted that the sale, for which contracts had been exchanged in September 1976, was followed by protracted litigation by third parties who claimed an interest in the ships. Cunard expected to make a 'modest profit' on its two-year charter

to Salen, but after that anticipated a substantial increase in charter rates for reefers, due to the decline in new buildings since 1974 and the scrapping of older vessels.

In Cunard service

Cunard's purchase involved three types of ships, which had carried distinct naming schemes under Maritime Fruit Carriers. Four were the Smith's Dock-built clippers, given names beginning with the letter A. The smallest of the three types, these were to a design produced by the Drammen yard in Norway. They were valued at $6.9 million each. The two Cs, *Carinthia* and *Carmania,* were to a larger design, Norwegian-built and which originally carried names of fruits, and were valued at $9.4 million each. The four largest, valued at $11.4 million each, were given names beginning S. They had come from a Danish yard and had been named after flowers. The ten ships were valued at $92 million, so for $86 million Cunard were getting a good deal.

Several of the ships had been laid up, some on the River Blackwater in Essex, and they were sent to Falmouth for overhaul. Top is *Gladiola* dry docked at Falmouth in November 1976. As *Saxonia* she initially retained the white hull but with red boot topping, as seen in the middle photograph on the Nieuw Waterweg in June 1977. Views of the reefers with Cunard's funnel colours are surprisingly rare, but *Saxonia* was photographed, left, in dry dock at North Shields in 1982. [*World Ship Photo Library 74061; David Salisbury; World Ship Photo Library 40958*]

Above: *Iris Queen* at Falmouth in November 1976 about to enter dry dock after being bought by Cunard. She emerged as *Scythia,* seen below in June 1979. *[World Ship Photo Library 24063 and 40959]*

There was much satisfaction expressed that Cunard was reviving its traditional names, especially after the unimaginative corporate names given to its bulkers. However, it was to be some time before Cunard funnel colours were to be carried, as Salen's ubiquitous blue funnel continued to be worn. Initially, the ships kept their white hulls, but were later painted grey. As the accompanying photos show, this was easier to keep looking smart.

In November 1979 all ten reefers were chartered for two years to United Brands, the US corporation probably better known under its earlier title of United Fruit. Amongst its subsidiaries were Fyffes and, some would argue, several small countries in Central America, for which the term 'banana republic' was coined. It would

seem that the four smallest Smith's Dock-built reefers did not prove economic under the British flag, and in July 1981 these were sold together with the remainder of the United Brands charter to the Greek Restis group for $6.5 million each. Even with inflation, this represented a good deal on ships that five years earlier had been valued at $6.9 million and bought by Cunard for less.

In November 1984 *Carinthia* took part in NATO exercise 'Ocean Safari' which involved a group of merchant ships being formed into a convoy and escorted down a narrow channel which had notionally been swept for mines by the Royal Navy. During the exercise the Navy monitored the performance of the merchant ships, noting their manoeuvrability, turning circles and stopping distance.

Above: *Servia* in the Nieuw Waterweg in August 1978. *[David Salisbury]*

One of the saddest of the many sad sights the author remembers on Merseyside in the early 1980s was a raft of reefers bearing classic Cunard names laid up in Vittoria Dock, Birkenhead. Paul Boot photographed them as, over the weeks of December 1985, they were gradually renamed, lost their Cunard funnels and sailed for new owners. The two photographs below show (upper) the scene on 8th December, with *Servia* recently renamed *Castor,* and (lower) a week later with *Castor* having left to reveal *Scythia* and others packing the dock behind her.

[Paul Boot]

After Cunard

In June 1985, the six reefers remaining with Cunard were laid up in a group in Vittoria Dock, Birkenhead, having concluded their charters and being put on the market. Kappa Maritime bought all six, and they stayed together, despite the changes in registered ownership, in manager's title, in flag and even in name which are endemic under Greek disponent ownership. Of a group which seemed remarkably trouble free in their early years, it is noteworthy that three of the four largest reefers, the S group in Cunard ownership, had major mishaps which left them fit only for scrap. Two had fires off the US eastern seaboard within the space of a few months in 1989, whilst the third, the former *Saxonia* by then named *Carina,* had such a forceful collision with a container ship in the North Sea during 1995 that tugs had to be called to pull the two apart.

In contrast, the four smaller reefers disposed of by Cunard in 1991 had a succession of owners, who typically bought and then quite quickly sold them in pairs. They began to go for scrap in 1994. Their frequently changing ownership and briefer careers than the three larger ships which survived marine hazards suggests that the four British-built reefers did not prove such good investments.

It would need intimate study of the accounts of Trafalgar House to know whether the ten Cunard reefers proved as good investments as they seemed in 1976. At the very least, the nine years' service which the six larger ships gave to Cunard helped keep the company's cargo ship tradition alive, and succeeded in 'providing continuing employment for British seamen'.

Fleet list

ALAUNIA 1976-1981

O.N. 361584 4,938g 2,636n 7,689d 461.5 x 60.3 x 38.1 feet
Sulzer type oil engine 9-cyl. 2SCSA by George Clark and
North Eastern Marine Engineering Co. Ltd., Wallsend;
14,850 BHP, 23 knots.

6.3.1973: Launched by Smith's Dock Co. Ltd., South Bank,
Middlesbrough (Yard No.1323) as CARDIFF CLIPPER.
6.1973: Completed for Cardigan Bay Shipping Co. Ltd.,
London (Maritime Fruit Carriers Co. Ltd., Haifa, Israel).
1974: Owners became Abeyreuth Shipping Co. Ltd. and
Adelaide Shipping Lines Ltd., London (Maritime Fruit
Carriers Co. Ltd., Haifa, Israel).
1976: Acquired by the Cunard Steam-ship Co. Ltd.
(Cunard-Brocklebank Ltd., managers), London and
renamed ALAUNIA.
1981: Sold to Amorgos Maritime Co. S.A., Panama
(Enterprises Shipping and Trading S.A. (S. Restis), Piraeus,
Greece) and renamed OCEANIA FREEZER under the
Greek flag.
1986: Sold to Laval Maritime Ltd., Monrovia, Liberia
(Enterprises Shipping and Trading S.A. (S. Restis), Piraeus,
Greece) and renamed FROSTY under the Greek flag.
1987: Sold to Acefrosty Navigation Co. Ltd., Valletta, Malta
(Government of Cuba, Havana) and renamed ACE
FROSTY.
1988: Sold to Mazatlan Shipping Co. Ltd., Limassol,
Cyprus (Laskaridis Shipping Co. Ltd., Piraeus, Greece) and
renamed FRIO BREMEN.
1993: Owners became Lilium Maritime S.A., Panama
(Laskaridis Shipping Co. Ltd., Piraeus, Greece).
1994: Sold to UB Shipping Ltd. (Ugland Interocean
Management Ltd.), London and renamed GOLDEN B under
the Panama flag.
1996: Sold to Ugland Reefers Ltd. (Ugland International
Holdings plc), Grand Cayman, Cayman Islands.
1997: Renamed UB PEARL.
2.11.1998: Arrived Alang to be broken up having been sold
to Global Investors Ltd.

ALSATIA 1976-1981

O.N. 357471 4,938g 2,636n 7,722d 461.5 x 60.3 x 38.1 feet
Sulzer type oil engine 9-cyl. 2SCSA by George Clark and
North Eastern Marine Engineering Co. Ltd., Wallsend;
14,850 BHP, 23 knots.

19.1.1972: Launched by Smith's Dock Co. Ltd., South Bank,
Middlesbrough (Yard No. 1318) for Chichester Shipping
Lines Ltd., North West Shipping Co. Ltd. and Island Fruit
Shipping Co. Ltd., London (Maritime Fruit Carriers Co. Ltd.,
Haifa, Israel) as EDINBURGH CLIPPER.
1976: Acquired by the Cunard Steam-ship Co. Ltd.
(Cunard-Brocklebank Ltd., managers), London and
renamed ALSATIA.
1981: Sold to Alaska Maritime Co. S.A., Panama
(Enterprises Shipping and Trading S.A. (S. Restis), Piraeus,
Greece) and renamed AMERICA FREEZER under the
Greek flag.
1985: Sold to Daiko Shipping Ltd., Monrovia, Liberia
(Enterprises Shipping and Trading S.A. (S. Restis), Piraeus,
Greece) and renamed ANGELMAR under the Greek flag.
1990: Sold to Nema Compania Naviera S.A., Panama
(Transcontinental Maritime and Trading S.A., Piraeus,
Greece) and renamed ATLANTICO under the Bahamas flag.
1990: Sold to Lucida Navigation S.A., Panama
(Transcontinental Maritime and Trading S.A., Piraeus,
Greece) and renamed NETWORK SWAN under the
Bahamas flag.
1991: Sold to Del-Monte Fresh Fruit (International) Ltd.
Monrovia, Liberia (Irgens Larsen A/S, Oslo, Norway,
managers).
1992: Owners became Del-Monte Fresh Fruit
(International) Ltd., Panama City, Panama (Network
Shipping Ltd., Coral Gables, Florida, managers) (Irgens
Larsen A/S, Oslo, Norway).
1992: Ultimate owners became Del-Monte Fresh Fruit
International Ltd., Hamilton, Bermuda and renamed
BANANA REEFER.
2.9.1994: Arrived in Chittagong Roads following sale to
breakers.
23.9.1994: Demolition began by Diamond Steel Products
Co. (Private) Ltd. at Bhatiary, Bangladesh.

Alaunia. [Author's collection]

ANDANIA 1976-1981

O.N. 357490 4,938g 2,636n 7,742d 461.5 x 60.3 x 38.1 feet
Sulzer type oil engine 9-cyl. 2SCSA by George Clark and
North Eastern Marine Engineering Co. Ltd., Wallsend;
14,850 BHP, 23 knots.

11.6.1972: Launched by Smith's Dock Co. Ltd., South
Bank, Middlesbrough (Yard No. 1320) for Sovertur
Shipping Co. Ltd., North West Shipping Co. Ltd. and Island
Fruit Shipping Co. Ltd., London (Maritime Fruit Carriers
Co. Ltd., Haifa, Israel) as GLASGOW CLIPPER.

1976: Acquired by the Cunard Steam-ship Co. Ltd.
(Cunard-Brocklebank Ltd., managers), London and
renamed ANDANIA

1981: Sold to Acadimos Maritime Co. S.A., Panama
(Enterprises Shipping and Trading S.A. (S. Restis), Piraeus,
Greece) and renamed EUROPE FREEZER under the Greek
flag.

1986: Sold to Ribarosa Shipping Ltd., Monrovia, Liberia
(Enterprises Shipping and Trading S.A. (S. Restis), Piraeus,
Greece) and renamed BALMAR under the Greek flag.

1990: Sold to Ultima Compania Naviera S.A., Panama
(Transcontinental Maritime and Trading S.A., Piraeus,
Greece) and renamed PACIFICO under the Bahamas flag.

1990: Sold to Oriental Galaxy S.A., Panama
(Transcontinental Maritime and Trading S.A., Piraeus,
Greece) and renamed NETWORK STORK under the
Bahamas flag.

1991: Sold to Del-Monte Fresh Fruit (International) Ltd.
Monrovia, Liberia (Irgens Larsen A/S, Oslo, Norway,
managers).

1992: Owners became Del-Monte Fresh Fruit
(International) Ltd., Panama City, Panama (Network
Shipping Ltd., Coral Gables, Florida, managers) (Irgens
Larsen A/S, Oslo, Norway).

1992: Ultimate owners became Del-Monte Fresh Fruit
International Ltd., Hamilton, Bermuda and renamed
BANANA PLANTER under the Panama flag.

14.1.1995: Laid up at Malalag Bay.

29.4.1995: Beached at Alang.

14.5.1995: Demolition began by Virat Shipbreaking
Corporation.

ANDRIA 1976-1981

O.N. 357505 4,938g 2,636n 7,689d 461.5 x 60.3 x 38.1 feet
Sulzer type oil engine 9-cyl. 2SCSA by George Clark and
North Eastern Marine Engineering Co. Ltd., Wallsend;
14,850 BHP, 23 knots

20.11.1972: Launched by Smith's Dock Co. Ltd., South
Bank, Middlesbrough (Yard No. 1321) for Curtis Shipping
Co. Ltd. and others, London (Maritime Fruit Carriers Co.
Ltd., Haifa, Israel) as TEESSIDE CLIPPER.

1976: Acquired by the Cunard Steam-ship Co. Ltd.
(Cunard-Brocklebank Ltd., managers), London and
renamed ANDRIA

1981: Sold to Akropol Navigation Co. S.A., Panama
(Enterprises Shipping and Trading S.A. (S. Restis), Piraeus,
Greece) and renamed AUSTRALIA FREEZER under the
Greek flag.

1986: Sold to Rubisun Marine S.A., Monrovia, Liberia
(Enterprises Shipping and Trading S.A. (S. Restis), Piraeus,
Greece) and renamed ACECHILLY under the Greek flag.

1988: Sold to Durango Shipping Co. Ltd., Limassol, Cyprus
(Laskaridis Shipping Co. Ltd., Piraeus, Greece) and
renamed FRIO HAMBURG.

1993: Sold to Marine Shield S.A., Panama (Laskaridis
Shipping Co. Ltd., Piraeus, Greece).

1994: Sold to UB Shipping Ltd. (Ugland Interocean
Management Ltd.), London and renamed BANANOR under
the Panama flag.

1996: Sold to Ugland Reefers Ltd. (Ugland International
Holdings plc), Grand Cayman, Cayman Islands.

1998: Renamed UB PRUDENT.

12.1998: Sold to Green Navigation Ltd. (Star Entech Ltd.),
St. Vincent and renamed PRIDE III.

17.1.1999: Arrived at Mumbai to be broken up.

Opposite top:
Andania
[J.K. Byass]

Opposite bottom:
Andria. Apart from the position of the fleet name on the bridge and the degrees of rust stain, these Smith's Dock-built reefers were identical.

Right: *Carinthia.*
[Ships in Focus]

CARINTHIA 1976-1985
O.N. 361582 7,330g 3,542n 9,551d 511.2 x 70.1 x 41.7 feet
Oil engine 9-cyl. 2SCSA by Nylands M/V, Oslo; 17,400 BHP, 20 knots.
19.1.1973: Launched by Nylands Verksted, Oslo (Yard No. 655) for Sagar Shipping Co. Ltd., London as CANTALOUP.
7.1973: Completed for Druidstan Ltd. (I.F.R. Services Ltd., managers), London (Maritime Fruit Carriers Co. Ltd., Haifa, Israel).
1976: Acquired by the Cunard Steam-ship Co. Ltd. (Cunard-Brocklebank Ltd., managers), London and renamed CARINTHIA
1985: Sold to Arlen Shipping Corporation, Monrovia, Liberia (Kappa Maritime Ltd. (G. and P.E. Kollakis), London) and renamed PEGASUS under the Greek flag.
1994: Owners became Emperor Investment Corporation, Monrovia, Liberia (Chartworld Shipping Corporation, Piraeus, Greece (Kappa Maritime Ltd. (G. and P.E. Kollakis), London), managers) and renamed STAR LIGHT.
1995: Owners became Caparison Shipping Corporation, Monrovia, Liberia (Chartworld Shipping Corporation, Piraeus, Greece (Kappa Maritime Ltd. (G. and P.E. Kollakis), London), managers) and renamed PELAGOS under the Bahamas flag.
1997: Managers became Kosmos Maritime Ltd. (D. Kastellis, Nikolaos Haberis, Nikolaos Markou), London.
2.7.2000: Arrived at Alang to be broken up.

CARMANIA 1976-1985
O.N. 357467 7,323g 3,546n 9,561d 511.2 x 70.1 x 41.7 feet
Oil engine 9-cyl. 2SCSA by Nylands M/V, Oslo; 17,400 BHP, 22 knots.
19.11.1971: Launched by Nylands Verksted, Oslo (Yard No. 652) for Chichester Shipping Lines Ltd. (I.F.R. Services Ltd., managers), London (Maritime Fruit Carriers Co. Ltd., Haifa, Israel) as ORANGE.
3.1972: Completed.
1976: Acquired by the Cunard Steam-ship Co. Ltd. (Cunard-Brocklebank Ltd., managers), London and renamed CARMANIA
1985: Sold to Garton Shipping Corporation, Monrovia, Liberia (Kappa Maritime Ltd. (G. and P.E. Kollakis), London) and renamed PERSEUS under the Greek flag.
1995: Managers became Chartworld Shipping Corporation, Piraeus, Greece (Kappa Maritime Ltd. (G. and P.E. Kollakis), London), managers) under the Bahamas flag.
1997: Managers became Kosmos Maritime Ltd. (D. Kastellis, Nikolaos Haberis, Nikolaos Markou), London.
13.6.1999: Arrived at Alang to be broken up.

SAMARIA 1976-1986
O.N. 357499 12,059/8,577g 6,915/4,722n 575.3 x 75.0 x 44.3 feet
Oil engine 9-cyl. 2SCSA by Burmeister & Wain, Copenhagen; 23,200 BHP, 23.5 knots.
31.8.1972: Launched by Aalborg Vaerft A/S, Aalborg,

Denmark (Yard No. 198) for Paravon Shipping Co. Ltd., London (Maritime Fruit Carriers Co. Ltd., Haifa, Israel) as CHRYSANTEMA.
2.1973: Completed.
1976: Acquired by the Cunard Steam-ship Co. Ltd. (Cunard-Brocklebank Ltd., managers), London and renamed SAMARIA.
1986: Sold to Cepheus Shipping Corporation, Monrovia, Liberia (Kappa Maritime Ltd. (G. and P.E. Kollakis), London) and renamed CAPRICORN under the Greek flag.
1986: Owners became the Diamond Seal Shipping Co. Ltd, Limassol, Cyprus (Kappa Maritime Ltd. (G. and P.E. Kollakis), London).
1992: Owners became Daphnis Shipping Corporation, Monrovia, Liberia (Chartworld Shipping Corporation, Piraeus, Greece (Kappa Maritime Ltd. (G. and P.E. Kollakis), London), managers) and placed under the Bahamas flag.
1997: Managers became Kosmos Maritime Ltd. (D. Kastellis, Nikolaos Haberis, Nikolaos Markou), London.
30.7.1997: Arrived at Alang to be broken up by Gupta Steel.

SAXONIA 1976-1985
O.N. 357465 12,029/8,547g 6,900/4,706n 575.3 x 75.0 x 44.3 feet
Oil engine 9-cyl. 2SCSA by Burmeister & Wain, Copenhagen; 23,200 BHP, 23.5 knots.
2.6.1971: Launched by Aalborg Vaerft A/S, Aalborg, Denmark (Yard No. 195) for Adelaide Shipping Lines Ltd., London (Maritime Fruit Carriers Co. Ltd., Haifa, Israel) as GLADIOLA.
2.1972: Completed.
1976: Acquired by the Cunard Steam-ship Co. Ltd. (Cunard-Brocklebank Ltd., managers), London and renamed SAXONIA
1985: Sold to Cepheus Tondo Shipping Corporation, Monrovia, Liberia (Kappa Maritime Ltd. (G. and P.E. Kollakis), London) and renamed CARINA under the Greek flag.
1986: Owners became Skyrocket Shipping Co. Ltd., Limassol, Cyprus (Kappa Maritime Ltd. (G. and P.E. Kollakis), London).
1992: Owners became Chloe Shipping Corporation, Monrovia, Liberia (Chartworld Shipping Corporation, Piraeus, Greece (Kappa Maritime Ltd., London), managers) and later placed under the Bahamas flag.
7.7.1995: Damaged in collision with the Panamanian motor container ship MSC SAMIA (40,944/1973) in position 51.22.05 north by 02.46.00 east whilst on a voyage from Bellingham to Vlissingen with a cargo of potato chips. The vessels were separated by tugs and CARINA was taken to Zeebrugge, arriving on 18.7.1995, and was later declared a constructive total loss.
18.3.1996: Demolition began at Alliaga by Dortel Gemi Sokum Demir Celik at Aliaga, Turkey.

SCYTHIA 1976-1985

O.N. 357489 12,059/8,557g 6,915/4,772n 575.3 x 75.0 x 44.3 feet

Oil engine 9-cyl. 2SCSA by Burmeister & Wain, Copenhagen; 23,200 BHP, 23.5 knots.

23.5.1972: Launched by Aalborg Vaerft A/S, Aalborg, Denmark (Yard No. 197) for Adelaide Shipping Lines Ltd., London (Maritime Fruit Carriers Co. Ltd., Haifa, Israel) as IRIS QUEEN.

11.1972: Completed.

1976: Acquired by the Cunard Steam-ship Co. Ltd. (Cunard-Brocklebank Ltd., managers), London and renamed SCYTHIA.

1985: Sold to Toulon Shipping Corporation, Monrovia, Liberia (Kappa Maritime Ltd. (G. and P.E. Kollakis), London) and renamed CENTAURUS under the Greek flag.

1989: Owners became Skyhope Shipping Co. Ltd., Limassol, Cyprus (Kappa Maritime Ltd. (G. and P.E. Kollakis), London).

8.2.1989: Abandoned after fire broke out at Wilmington, Delaware whilst on a voyage from Honduras to Wilmington with a cargo of bananas. Towed out to sea later that day, fire extinguished, and towed in again by 18.2.1989. Declared a constructive total loss

16.7.1989: Arrived Chittagong.

20.7.1989: Demolition began by Abdul Motaleb.

SERVIA 1976-1985

O.N. 357481 12,059/8,577g 6,920/4,722n 575.3 x 75.0 x 44.3 feet

Oil engine 9-cyl. 2SCSA by A/S Burmeister & Wain's Motor-og Mfbk af 1971, Copenhagen; 23,200 BHP, 24 knots.

7.1972: Completed by Aalborg Vaerft A/S, Aalborg, Denmark (Yard No. 196) for Austral Shipping Lines Ltd., London (Maritime Fruit Carriers Co. Ltd., Haifa, Israel) as ORCHIDEA.

1976: Acquired by the Cunard Steam-ship Co. Ltd. (Cunard-Brocklebank Ltd., managers), London and renamed SERVIA

1985: Sold to Iaco Shipping Corporation, Monrovia, Liberia (Kappa Maritime Ltd. (G. and P.E. Kollakis), London) and renamed CASTOR under the Greek flag.

1987: Owners became Gold Seal Shipping Co. Ltd., Limassol, Cyprus (Kappa Maritime Ltd. (G. and P.E. Kollakis), London) and renamed KASTORA.

26.4.1989: Fire broke out in engine room and engine room flooded in position 15.08 north by 74.20 west whilst on a voyage from Puerto Limon, Costa Rica to New Orleans with a cargo of bananas.

29.4.1989: Towed in after fire extinguished. Subsequently declared a constructive total loss and sold for demolition.

31.3.1990: Demolition began by M.H. and Company (Private) Ltd. at Gadani Beach.

Above: *Servia.*
[M.D.J. Lennon]

Right: As a postscript, this is another of the Smith's Dock-built reefers which remained British after the Maritime Fruit Carriers' collapse. Blue Star's *Trojan Star* was formerly *Newcastle Clipper.* As with Cunard's 'A' class, her new buyers did not keep her long, and she remained with Blue Star only until 1980 when she was sold to become *Chios Clipper.*
[J. and M. Clarkson collection]

PUTTING THE RECORD STRAIGHT

Letters, additions, amendments and photographs relating to articles in any issues of *Record* are welcomed. Letters may be lightly edited. E-mails are welcome, but senders are asked to include their postal address.

The short feature on Lobnitz, 'Renfrew Retrospective', in Record 26 brought forth an unprecedented amount of additional material from Derek Atherton, Bill Lind and William Turrell. As explained in the Introduction, we are short of space for scheduled articles in this issue, and - with apologies to these contributors - the follow-up on Lobnitz has been postponed. Similarly, several letters have been held over for future issues.

From Donaghadee to 'Derry

I was intrigued by the references (*Record* 26, page 93) to the Donaghadee gun-running of April 1914, and whether John S. Paton the owner of the *Innismurray* would have known what his vessel was being used for. As Samuel Kelly was heavily involved, his steamer *Balmarino* acting effectively as a decoy, flashing lights and approaching her berth at Belfast extremely slowly, while the coaster *Roma* (Howdens, Larne) actually slipped in with guns, I always imagined Paton must have been enlisted. These coastal shipowners all knew each other. However, on re-reading accounts of the events, I am not so sure. When the *Innismurray* arrived in Larne to take guns from the *Clyde Valley* on to Donaghadee - while the *Roma* was similarly loaded for Belfast - there occurred the only hitch in the anti-Home Rulers' plans. The crew of the *Innismurray* were found to be mainly Nationalists, i.e. of the opposite political persuasion to the gun-runners! Volunteers were hastily assembled to take the *Innismurray* on to Donaghadee. One wonders if the crucial knowledge to operate the Bolinders engine was there.

A week afterwards the *Innismurray* was detained by the Customs at Drogheda, but there was little attempt to take any steps against those involved in the whole operation,

The scene at Donaghadee during the gun-running episode referred to in Ian Wilson's letter: the charabanc can be seen and, less clearly, the *Innismurray*. [The Ulster Society, courtesy North Down Heritage Centre]

no doubt in part because such numbers of influential figures in Irish life - and elsewhere in the British Isles - were sympathetic. The attitudes of today cannot be applied to a vanished era. But the onset of the First World War served to, almost literally, defuse the Irish situation - for a time.

I enclose a copy of a rare photograph showing the operation at Donaghadee. The mast and bridge of the *Innismurray* can be seen. The charabanc reminds me that this is said to be the first complex military operation in history using organised motor vehicle transport.

On another point in the same issue, the William Mitchell, after whom the square-rigger was named, was in fact the principal of the Foyle Line of Londonderry, her owners. He had five deep-sea vessels built at Bigger's yard in the city: *Foyledale, Alexander Black, William Tilley, John Cook* and *William Mitchell*. Sadly, Mitchell was accidentally drowned at Warrenpoint, County Down, on 10th July 1902, after which the fleet was sold off. A short chapter on the Foyle Line appears in 'Sailing Ships of Ireland' by Ernest B. Anderson (Dublin, Morris and Co., 1951 - facsimile reprint Impact, Ballycastle, County Antrim, 1985).
IAN WILSON, Manager, North Down Heritage Centre, Town Hall, The Castle, Bangor, County Down BT20 4BT

Sobriquets sought

It might be a good idea to use your readers to compile a list of nicknames for the various shipping companies before these are lost in time. 'Blue Flue', 'Hungry Hogarths', 'Ropey Ropners', 'Shaw Swivel', 'two of fat and one of lean' (T. and J. Harrison), 'silver banders' (Stephenson Clark), 'Crazy (Cayzer) Gang', 'Lavender Hull Mob' (Union-Castle) are a few of the repeatable ones I remember when I was deep sea.
A.D. FROST, 32 Oakfield Close, Sunderland SR3 3RT
The initials SSA (officially Shaw, Savill and Albion) were interpreted as 'Slow Starvation and Agony'. Ed.

The Big Ics

The article in *Record* 24 by Captain Edward Buckle brought back a host of memories, particularly of Captain Buckle with whom I sailed as cadet, second officer and chief officer. The various photographs of *Ceramic* and *Gothic* are interesting in that several (pages 198, 202 and 233) clearly show that the louvres of the Thorneycroft funnel top have been removed. I have photographs taken during my voyage in 1966 which show them missing from *Ceramic* at that time. I imagine that they corroded and were removed for safety reasons but were not replaced as it would have been an expensive exercise.

The caption for *Athenic* on page 232 says that she has lost one of her pairs of lifeboats but there is a lifeboat sitting on deck abreast number 5 hatch. This must have been a temporary stow while undergoing survey and/or repair without passengers on board while coasting in UK waters.

Your comments about the selection of officers for the Royal Tour are interesting but it would seem that Captain Aitchison was not the first choice master as Captain A.V. Richardson was in command for the abandoned tour. However, he retired at the end of July 1953 and the honour fell to Captain Aitchison.

Fifty years ago, *Gothic* was serving as the Royal Yacht for the Royal Commonwealth Tour and it is pleasing to report that a Bassett Lowke waterline model of her as the Royal Yacht is now displayed on board HQS *Wellington*, the floating livery hall of the Honourable Company of Master Mariners, having been given on permanent loan by Furness Withy and Co. Ltd. through the Shaw Savill Society in June 2001.
GRAHAM PEPPER, Lantern Cottage, Church Lane, Ford End, Essex CM3 ILH

Oxford to *Karachi* via *Boston*

The riddle of the portholes and extra lifeboats in number 5 upper 'tween decks on both the *City of Oxford* and *City of Birmingham* (*Record* 27, page 176) is quite simply explained in that those ships were used to ferry Indian crews to and from USA or UK and Bombay or Calcutta. There was accommodation for about 100 Indian crew members in cabins of eight and in the mast house of the mainmast there were toilet/bathroom facilities for the extra crew and also an extra crew galley, as each deck and engine crew carried had their own bhandary. Stewards, as there were so few of them, tended to mess with the vessel's own crew. With so many extra crew on board the extra lifeboats were necessary, but on occasions were removed. With regular services on the UK/South African trades and also MANZ Line, as well as Wilson's transatlantic ships, there were considerable numbers of Ellerman crews to be taken home after they had finished their time on board their own ships. It was always fun, as by then they had always accumulated a considerable number of bicycles, sewing machines or other large major items that were unavailable in India.

The *City of Oxford* was built by John Brown at Clydebank and is the next yard number to Cunard's *Caronia* and it was often said that Brown's apprentices built the *City of Oxford* and the skilled tradesmen built the *Caronia*. In fact there were several bits and pieces of fittings on the *City of Oxford* that had been built for the *Caronia* - such as the engine room desk - a large and elaborate affair, much grander than any desk in any of the other engine-rooms fitted to vessels of the *City of Oxford* class. Several other pieces of furniture also were more typical of Cunard than of Ellerman.

The photograph at the foot of page 176 was taken by Moffat-Scott on 29th December 1954 when we were leaving Capetown bound for Port Elizabeth. Why I am convinced the photograph is of that day is that it clearly shows the Clark Chapman winch at number 2A hatch with a canvas cover and this was only done on one occasion. Also the ship's temporary swimming pool is rigged on the port side, alongside number 4 hatch; whereas normally it was rigged on the starboard side. Both these changes were made for the outward voyage from UK to South Africa when we carried Sir John Ellerman and his friends to winter in the warmth of that country. Indeed the *City of Oxford* had been virtually converted into Sir John's private yacht by Barclay Curle at Elderslie for the voyage. I have many happy memories of that voyage and the Christmas on board, for as a raw 16-year-old cadet I was not used to mixing in such exalted company. Whilst the ship had little commercial cargo on board the reason for the switch in sides of the swimming pool was that we had loaded a 120-ton steam locomotive under Finieston Crane in Glasgow, where the deck was strengthened and the starboard side lifeboat removed and stowed in the lower 'tween decks.

It seems a shame that there is no Ellerman Association to keep these memories alive. Part of this I believe is the lack of camaraderie in Ellermans, partly caused by having their cadets indentured to either City Line, Hall Line or Ellerman and Bucknall and not offering staff a contract until they obtained their master's or chief engineer's certificates. It did not do a lot to inspire loyalty in the junior officers and engineers.
CAPTAIN DAVE VINCENT, Matupit Cottage, 7 High Street, Puddletown, Dorset DT2 8RT

The photograph of *City of Birkenhead* at the base of page 178 in *Record* 27 was taken in Boston. Indeed I can date it to 3rd May 1969 and very probably taken by my father. I have a negative taken perhaps about 10 seconds later by which time the aircraft in the view had reached a point aft of the *City of Birkenhead's* mainmast. The tug in the foreground is a give-away - *Orion* of Boston Towboat Company - one of three sisters - *Juno* and *Triton* being the other two, which were the backbone of Boston Tow's fleet for nearly twenty years. The photo is taken from Castle Island at the mouth of Boston's inner harbour, a superb vantage point used by ship photographers as far back as 1910. Boston's Logan International Airport lies diagonally opposite on the other side of the channel, which does make it a noisy location. If the wind is right the landing pattern brings large jets in about 500 feet overhead. Fortunately, the Massachusetts Air National Guard Fighter Squadron which

was once stationed at Logan is gone. The roar of a pair of fighters revving up on after-burner at the near end of the runway was a head-splitting feature of Saturday and Sunday afternoons at Castle Island in the 1960s. That the *City of Birkenhead* has already taken a tug off Castle Island indicates that she will berth at the adjacent Castle Island Terminal, now the Conley Container Terminal.
BILL SCHELL, 334 South Franklin Street, Holbrook, MA 02343, USA

Comments and corrections to *Record* 27
Page 133: Only the Ardrossan ships had Kincaid-built engines. All the others had their engine built in Harland and Wolff's own Glasgow works.
Page 141: For G.R. Glover, read G.R. Clover.
Page 181, *City of Singapore:* surely the boats by the mainmast are in the lower photo as well?
BILL LAXON, Waimarama, Upper Whangateau Road, PO Box 171, Matakana 1240, New Zealand.

Record 27 has a photo of the trooper *Huntsend* being attended by a tug identified as *Knight of St. John.* This attribution seems rather unlikely since Prendiville's *Knight of St. John* (1884), having passed briefly through Vincent Grech's hands, had been owned by the Ottoman Government since 1897 as *Samsun* and then was converted to a minelayer in 1914. She was torpedoed and sunk on 14th August 1915 by the British submarine E2 in the Sea of Marmara.
DAVID ASPREY, 60 Barnstaple Road, Thorpe Bay, Southend-on-Sea SS1 3PA
Can anyone put a name to this tug? The freighter in this feature is also still awaiting identification. Ed.

Sunderland revisited
Thanks to my old school friend David Aris (we sat next to each other in infant school drawing ships on our slates!) for the additional information (*Record* 27) concerning Doxford's shipbuilding and engine works, supplementing my comments in 'Sunderland in Focus 2' (*Record* 25). I fear, however, that he has been caught out by the same 'trick of light' which puzzled me when I first examined the three photographs which showed the Pallion premises in the 1930s. I am sure that, if he examines the right-hand picture on page 55 more closely, he will see that the fourth ship he refers to is actually inside the supports for the gantry cranes and is, therefore, the left-hand vessel of the three shown under construction in the left-hand photograph on page 55. The relative positions of the small boats in the river on all three photographs would also seem to confirm that the photographs are part of a sequence.
JOHN LINGWOOD, 52 Nursery Road, Sunderland SR3 INT
Thanks also to regular correspondent A.D. Frost of Sunderland, who confirms John's interpretation of the photograph. Ed.

Corabank voyage recalled
I was particularly interested in the Bank Line details (*Records* 17 and 18) because when I went back to sea in 1974 I had a wonderful round the world voyage on the *Corabank,* Captain Spen Lynch. We loaded on the continent to New Orleans (three weeks alongside in the French Quarter - those were the days when ships had derricks!) and after discharging there it was loading for a string of Pacific Islands, Australia, Tasmania and back via New Guinea and the Red Sea. The *Corabank* (illustrated opposite) was built for the trade with special tanks for palm oil and we picked up cocoa and copra from the islands. What a run! Around 1981 I joined her again for the same voyage. I saw her for the last time in Swansea, when she came in for repairs. It would be wonderful for me to hear from my old shipmates again, especially Spen Lynch (I have changed my name in the mean time).
JOANNA GREENLAW, 59 King Edward Road, Swansea SA1 4LN

Messageries matters

I wish to convey my greatest appreciation for your magazine, and congratulate you for this wonderful work. I also have some information regarding some earlier issues.

The name Messageries Maritimes stems from the origins of the company itself, in the coach and post business. Under the Old Regime, coach transport was franchised by the state to eight private companies (fermiers généraux) which were sometimes under private ownership, and sometimes under government control depending on the policy of the Finance Ministry. Then came the Revolution, giving the coach and post business over to private industry.

The Messageries Maritimes were formed as a coach business, by the amalgamation of two of those private companies, on 19 Thermidor An VI (which translates into 7th August 1798), with central offices in Rue Notre Dame des Victoires. Depending on the regime, the name was changed to Messageries Nationales, then Impèriales, and finally Royales in 1815.

Originally, it ran services to the south from Paris, with a water coach on the Saone: very modest beginnings indeed for a company whose network was to span the world.

There we have our first landmark: the crest of the original company was a horse, which progressively turned into a unicorn resting on an anchor, as a 'marinised' version of the animal.

Then came the industrial revolution; steam and railways spelled the end of the horse-drawn carriage for passengers. In 1850 the company, whilst still transporting a great number of passengers and spreading its network, had been driven out to the very outskirts of the country by rail. Clearly the writing was on the wall, and the board of directors decided on a bold move: bidding for maritime postal services in the Mediterranean, which had been hitherto run at a great deficit by the administration. The founding act of the new company was signed on 6th August 1851, the company inheriting old units of the postal service reinforced by the acquisition of the entire Rostand fleet. Initial services were to Algeria (which had been the subject of colonial conquest for 20 years) and Italy, but gradually looking east. As a measure of the independence of the new company, a state representative sat on the board of directors.

Our second and final landmark was the red-cornered flag: it was that of the initial postal service, but slightly modified: the initial P was replaced by MN (1851-52), then MI (1852-70) and finally MM (1870-1976), with the white central lozenge being greatly enlarged.

So contrary to Captain Kinghorn's belief, the name comes from coach services, and not from the zoo…

There is more on this in 'Sur les Routes de la Mer avec les Messageries Maritimes' by Roger Carour (Editions André Bonne, Paris, 1968)
Dr. JEAN PIERRE BUREL, 62 rue Théagène Boufart, 76400 Fécamp, France
Information provided by Dr. Rubel on the Fécamp trawlers referred to on page 59 of Record *25 has been held over to a forthcoming issue.*

Dockers on the Scotch

It was with great pleasure I read Graeme Somner's history of London Scottish Lines in *Record* 27. I would like to correct one minor error: the master of the *Edinburgh Merchant* was Captain T.S. Robertson, not Robinson. In 1940 Captain Robertson was at Dunkirk with the *Scottish Co-operator* as she then was. After unloading, Captain Robertson on his own initiative took the ship alongside a jetty and, under fire, evacuated 500 troops.

I served on the *Edinburgh Merchant* from June 1957 to January 1959, when she was put up for sale. As Graeme Somner states, the demise of the company was due, in no small part, to the frequent stoppages of work by London dockers. I well remember the occasion when the crew's prospect of Christmas at home was wrecked by the dockers' decision to unload our cargo of export whisky one case at a time due to some dispute.

I was at the wheel when the *Edinburgh Merchant* collided with the *Pass of Glenogle* near the Dudgeon Light vessel. It was during thick fog and we had no radar. Fortunately, the sea was calm and damage was confined to the upper part of the port bow and the crew accommodation aft. There were no casualties.

The vehicles shown as deck cargo in the photographs were Ford vans and cars, presumably built at Dagenham and shipped north to dealers in Edinburgh. On another occasion our deck cargo consisted of a very grumpy lion and a giraffe en route to Edinburgh Zoo.
WILLIAM LORIMER, 6 Antonine Court, Bo'Ness, West Lothian EH51 0ND

Cycles and lighters

A brief note to support your editorial decision to revert the frequency of *Record* from quarterly to its original four-month cycle. The arrival of *Record* is always something to be eagerly anticipated and fully savoured so any form of short rations is to be deplored. However, if missing one issue in a year is declared necessary to maintain production standards then so be it. I fully appreciate that *Record* will always be marginally commercial and so I support any measure that enables it to survive. The appearance of any issue in book standard quality at the cover price of a bog-standard paperback remains a good deed in a dark world and I sincerely hope that this change you have introduced guarantees that it'll go on illuminating for many years yet.

As an old West Coast hand, I enjoyed the Elder Dempster 'Explorer' class feature, albeit all the ships were before my time. One small point: in the photograph at the top of page 136, the forward jumbo derrick of the *David Livingstone* looks distinctly unequal to the challenge of the deck cargo. But, as it resembles one of those many cargo lighters that were still doing sterling service in the creeks of the Niger Delta for decades after they were delivered, I suppose they must have persuaded it off the foredeck somehow!
JOHN GOBLE, 55 Shanklin Road, Southampton SO15 7RG

The six Swan Hunter-built ships for Bank Line, beginning with *Corabank* (11,405/1973), prompted the photographer to write on the back of this print 'at least someone is still building decent-looking ships!' *Corabank* remained with Bank Line only until 1984, and then served as the Peruvian *Unicosta* and the Singapore-owned *Kota Berani* until broken up at Alang in 1993. [M.R. Dippy]

PORTS AND HARBOURS OF COUNTY DOWN
Ian Wilson

Of all the coastal counties in Ireland, I would suggest County Down had the greatest number of commercial harbours, quays and open discharging beaches. Cork perhaps runs it close. In 1900, I would estimate there were at least 25 places where one could see cargo being handled. The reasons for this were complex: the demands of a relatively populous and prosperous hinterland and its need for export channels for farm produce; the incomplete railway system; the proximity of Scotland, north west England and the Isle of Man; the sheltered nature of many of the coastal villages in a heavily indented coastline; and the difficulty of moving heavy loads before the advent of the motor lorry. The most important truism in studying coastal trade is that, until relatively recently, it was always the case that heavy goods were moved by water from as near as possible to their point of origin to as near as possible to their destination. Thus it is wrong to think of navigating a small sailing ship through the rocky narrows into

Strangford Lough and then through winding channels to Ballydorn quay as 'difficult' - it was the only way things had ever been done. Before the age of photography, deep-sea vessels with American grain came right up Strangford Lough on the tide to its shallow upper reaches and discharged into barges. These negotiated a narrow muddy river and supplied the huge flour mill in Comber of the merchant princes, the Andrews family, of which Thomas Andrews, designer of the *Titanic* was a later member. Nowadays this would be considered unthinkable, laughable even, but in 1850 it was perfectly logical!

Today's visitor to the scenic coast will find that very little has been spoiled by progress. Quite a number of stretches of the coastline are owned by the National Trust. Housing on the quays of Dundrum and Killyleagh certainly jars, but there are still any number of old quays and harbours where, thankfully, little has changed from the days of these photographs.

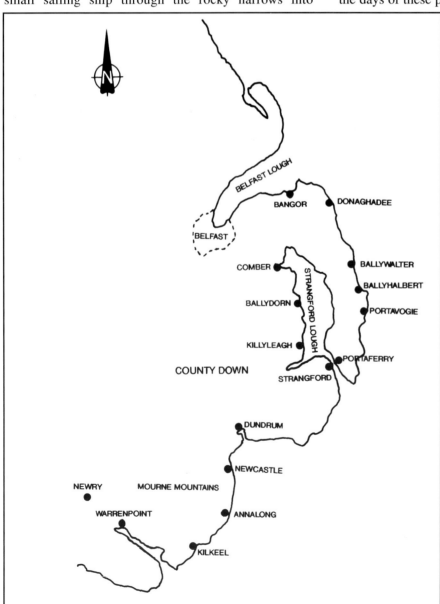

Left: Map of the County Down ports.

The *Reedness* at Ballydorn, Strangford Lough (opposite, top)
This truly marvellous postcard was published locally, and does turn up occasionally in dealers' boxes. It is an intensely evocative summer scene from about 1930. Ballydorn Quay, approached via a twisting channel between the picturesque islands of Strangford Lough, dates from the 1850s and served the small villages of Killinchy and Ardmillan and their rural environs, the staple cargoes being coal in and potatoes out. Motorists and their children have left their stately machines to take in the hiss and clatter of the ship's steam winch discharging into horse-drawn carts. The *Reedness* was built in 1903 as the *Brookside* for James Shiels of Belfast and narrowly survived grounding on the Down coast in 1905 when bound for Ardglass. Ultimately, in November 1938, she became a constructive total loss when, as Coe's *Redthorn,* she struck the River Bann bar while inward for Coleraine. This photograph was taken after Coe bought her in 1931, but before renaming in 1936. Today the former Tuskar Rock lightship *Petrel,* built at Dublin in 1916, makes an attractive sight adjacent to the old quay as the headquarters of Down Cruising Club. Local memory is that the last coaster berthed here about 1942.

[Author's collection]

The second *Cumbria* at Ballywalter (below)

The stone quay at Ballywalter is a substantial structure now by-passed by coastal shipping but, when built around 1854, of major importance to the district. Although vulnerable to easterly weather, Ballywalter harbour handled regular coal imports until September 1965, when the *Polarlight* made the final call. This 1921-built *Cumbria* replaced a similar, older steamer of the same name in the summer of 1955. Her master, Captain William Bennett of Killyleagh, County Down, was involved in the ownership with her manager, John B. Moffatt of Whitehaven. Moffatt had been the official owner of the previous *Cumbria* (ex-*Norrix*, ex-*Abus*), but Captain Bennett may well have had a stake in her, too. A master/owner set-up was very unusual in County Down after the passing of sail. Captain Bennett's father had begun in a small sailing barge in the sand trade within Strangford Lough, and rose to command the Killyleagh-owned schooners *Liffey Maid* and *Elizabeth Ellen Fisher.* After just two years this second *Cumbria,* acquired as the *Orkney Dawn* and built as the *Redesmere,* also ended up, like the first, in the destructive hands of the West of Scotland Shipbreaking Co. Ltd. at Troon. *[Author's collection]*

Donaghadee harbour, 1920s

This panoramic view was taken by the Ulster professional photographer William A. Green from the tower of the Parish Church. Donaghadee, just 20 miles from Portpatrick on the Galloway peninsula in Scotland, served for centuries as the Irish terminus of the mail route. With the coming of paddle steamers in 1824, this new harbour was developed and completed in 1837 to elegant designs by Sir John Rennie. Prosperity seemed assured with the arrival of the railway from Belfast in 1861, but a fatal combination of official dithering and railway politics, plus the limitations of the small Portpatrick harbour, saw Stranraer/Larne emerge as the long-term successor. Donaghadee was left with a splendid harbour, but bereft of its raison d'être. Attempts were periodically made to prove 'the short sea route' viable, the last a summer service by the paddler *Terrible* in 1891, but from then until cessation of trade in 1955, coasters importing coal or bricks were the only callers. The fine large ketch seen here could very well be the *Anna*, built by Williams of Portmadoc in 1895 for Thomas Shaw of Kircubbin, County Down, and owned in the 1920s by Captain Alex Adair of Portavogie, just 12 miles down the coast from Donaghadee. Nowadays the *Balmoral* calls most summers, pleasantly justifying again the creation of a passenger port in a very small town. [*William A. Green collection, Ulster Folk and Transport Museum*]

250

Newry about 1920: the passenger steamer *Iveagh*

The *Iveagh* of the Dundalk and Newry Steam Packet Company lies quietly in the Albert Basin, at the head of the ship canal to Carlingford Lough. Completed in 1892 by Inglis on the Clyde at a cost of £19,018, she was the first company vessel of steel construction, with triple-expansion engines and lit throughout by electricity. It may seem quaint today that passengers could sail direct to Ardrossan and Liverpool from a port forgotten by all commercial shipping since 1974 - but who would be better off, the *Iveagh* passengers dining in their oak-panelled saloon after they stepped aboard in their home town, or the neglected 'foot passengers' of today, having to reach Belfast or Larne docks by public transport and then queuing for a bacon roll in an unreliable aluminium pod? Even the cattle drovers had 'comfortable accommodation quite separate from that provided for livestock'. The *Iveagh* became the *Lady Iveagh* when her owners were taken over by the British and Irish Steam Packet Co. Ltd. in 1930, but was broken up soon after. The Dundalk and Newry firm had itself been the result of an alliance in 1871 between interests in the neighbouring ports. Visible beyond the steamer are barges trading on the inland stretch of the canal, and also what appears to be an auxiliary ketch. Thankfully, the lock gates where the ship canal meets the sea were kept maintained, and after 20 years Newry port has been revived by visits from the *Balmoral*, the Irish sail training brigantine *Asgard II* and smaller vessels.
[*William A. Green collection, Ulster Folk and Transport Museum*]

251

Low tide at Strangford: the Passing Cloud

As the official Belfast registry document for the *Passing Cloud* states, in copper-plate handwriting, 'sprang leak in the Irish Channel and lost 31 October 1923', this W.A. Green study must date from a summer's day just before that. *The Passing Cloud* was one of the last of a fleet of small sailing coasters which spent much of their time supplying the Belfast markets with farm produce. Thus the Belfast shipping arrivals for 1914 record: 30th January, *Passing Cloud*, Cully, from Ballyhalbert with beans and potatoes; 24th February, *Passing Cloud* from Portavogie with potatoes. Nowadays a few heavy lorries would take her cargo in 45 minutes! The skipper, John Cully of Portavogie, owned all 64 shares in the vessel, which had been built as a fishing boat by Henry Graves of Peel in 1884. The nomenclature of the rigs of these vessels is not worth getting pedantic about: essentially similar craft are referred to even in the official registry documents as 'lugger', 'dandy', 'smack', 'dandy smack', 'ketch', 'yawl', 'jigger' and 'sloop'! These Manx-built vessels were heavily influenced by West Cornish designs. Other Graves boats which passed into County Down cargo work included the *Rover's Belle*,

Lady Ventry, and *Ellen Shaw*. The ivy-clad sixteenth century tower once commanded the Narrows into Strangford Lough, and remains evidence of the strategic importance of the port of Strangford, which maintained a Customs establishment for centuries, to the English in Ulster. The last ship to use the historic harbour seems to have been the *Saint Oran*, which recorded four visits with coal in 1982.

[*William A. Green collection, Ulster Folk and Transport Museum*]

252

Portaferry, about 1900

Portaferry is the twin town of Strangford, a mile away across the Narrows. An interesting collection of vessels is captured by the camera of Robert Welch, the most prominent Ulster photogapher of the era. He has positioned himself here at the bows of a sailing vessel. The sixteenth-century tower shares command of the Narrows with its counterpart in Strangford. Portaferry was a surprisingly important shipbuilding town and port between about 1790 and 1840, and in 1802 the second-largest ship built in Ireland, the *Bess*, was launched here. Later, Newry and Belfast eclipsed Portaferry. On the left we see the smack *Vivid*, which changed her registry to Belfast in 1901. In November and December 1899, she is recorded as arriving five times at Belfast with wheat from Portaferry. An interesting contrast to the more shapely ex-fishing boat *Passing Cloud*, she too was Manx-built, by Qualtrough of Port St. Mary in 1863. Beside her is a queer craft. As Jim Blaney, a collector of oral history, recorded from John Bailie in 1972 '...the *Venture* belonged to Millar. It was built at the quay north west of the old church of Ardkeen. She was an awful-looking sight. She had a bow on her as broad as the coal quay. She had no propellor just a thing like a duck's foot that went in and out. She was made of wood and had an engine in her...' Was she a tug? Perhaps, but as this John Millar also owned the tiny 31-gross-ton wooden steamer *La Belle Marie*, a former Cardiff/Penarth ferry, and employed her carrying general cargo to and from Belfast, she probably did have a cargo hatch. The much more pleasing schooner seems to have all the characteristics of the many vessels built in Prince Edward Island. It is now about thirty years since a coaster called at Portaferry.

[*Welch collection, Ulster Museum*]

PORTAFERRY CASTLE FROM HARBOUR. R.W. 417

Reminders of a railway port: Dundrum, 1967

'One of the most interesting railway-connected harbours in the British Isles', comments railway historian R.M. Arnold in 'The County Down' (Whitehead, Co. Antrim, 1981). Sidings from the main Belfast to Newcastle line of the Belfast and County Down Railway extended down the quays belonging to the East Downshire Steamship Company, shipowners and coal and timber importers. Obviously tidal, the harbour was doubly handicapped by the long, winding approach across a treacherous sand bar. But until 1985, Dundrum was an active port. The large ruinous warehouse visible here was constructed in 1869, with the coming of the railway. The East Downshire firm owned a fleet of 10-ton wagons, painted in their livery, with which they distributed coal to various depots. The siding also handled potatoes for export in season, and sand, brought in from the bar by barges. But by October 1967, the date of this photograph, the railway had been closed for 17 years. The *Yarvic* had arrived in Dundrum earlier that year to run a general cargo service to Peel for new Kilkeel-based owner Nicholas Anley. However, this enterprise had its thunder stolen by a rival offering containerisation from Dundrum to Castletown, and the little *Yarvic*, originally the wartime *VIC 42* and lengthened in 1951, became for a time a coastal tramp, a throwback to the single-hatch small port traders of the past. In recent years, a cut-down remnant of the old warehouse has been transformed into 'prestigious' homes.   [*Author's collection*]

In the shadow of the Mournes: Annalong (opposite)

Annalong must be one of the prettiest harbours in the British Isles. The cameraman has his back to the open sea; the little dock was entered via a narrow outer basin. A very tight turn had to be effected, but once inside ships could be protected from any swell by baulks of timber lowered into slots by the crane seen right of centre. Mourne granite in the form of square setts and kerbstones was the main export up until 1939, and much of Liverpool was thus paved. Annalong was one of the last strongholds of sail, and up until the war years schooners such as the *Volant, Nellie Bywater* and *Lochranza Castle* gained increasing status as survivors of a passing age. The harbour was also very busy for about six years in the 1920s, when the massive civil engineering project of the Silent Valley Reservoir in the Mournes was under way. Rails for a light railway were imported, and ships of the Ramsey Steamship Company

brought tens of thousands of tons of coal and cement which were sent up the line, some of the coal being for the locomotives. Coppack's *Scotsman* frequently imported bricks. The steamer here is the *Jolly Frank* of London, just acquired by associates of the Ramsey firm and not yet renamed *Bradda*, which dates the photograph to the first six months of 1931. A ketch lies astern, and two fishing boats, types known locally as a skiff (left) and a nickey (right). After the war new materials superseded the need for granite on the roads, but sporadic cargoes of coal came until the early 1960s. In September 1970, the last cargo, salt, arrived on the small Bangor-owned *Schiestroom*. Annalong, with its corn mill seen here on the right now restored, is a delightful place to visit. As, indeed, is the whole County Down coastline. [*William A. Green collection, Ulster Folk and Transport Museum*]

Launch of the concrete barge *Creteforge*
It is 5th March 1919. Snow sprinkles the mountains overlooking Carlingford Lough as the *Creteforge* is launched sideways from the yard of J. and R. Thompson, Warrenpoint. In 1917, the Ministry of Munitions pressed the Admiralty for barges and tugs to bring iron ore from Spain, and suggested concrete owing to demands on steel. £4 million worth of vessels were ordered, often from small yards, and it was hoped unskilled labour could more readily be used with the concrete process. Thompson launched four barges between December 1918 and June 1919, in co-operation with the civil engineers McLaughlin and Harvey. Like many of her class, the *Creteforge* passed into the ownership of the Crete

Shipping Co. Ltd. (Stelp and Leighton Ltd., managers) and was sold to Spain in 1929. Virtually indestructible of course, quite a number of the tugs and barges still exist. Three are in Irish waters, two very near Warrenpoint in fact, the former tug *Cretegaff* and the barge *Cretefield*, which are now part of a marina off Carlingford town. Since 1937, the tug *Creteboom* has lain prominently in the estuary of the River Moy at Ballina, County Mayo. Both tugs were constructed at the forgotten yard of John ver Mehr, Shoreham. The reader interested in the concrete fleet and their fates is referred to the remarkable website www.mareud.mine.nu There really is a website for everything!

[*Hogg collection, Ulster Museum*]

256

SPYING ON SPAIN: 2

This is a second selection of photographs from what a postcard dealer described as a 'Scarce WW2 album of spy photographs of Spanish ships'. Compiled by British intelligence during the latter stages of the Second World War, it has many, mostly wartime, photographs taken from the water and from the air. This is a selection from the many freighters in the album. Note that the original prints, although of high quality, are rather closely cropped.

CABO ROCHE

Sociedad Española de Construcciones Naval, Bilbao; 1922, 2,776gt, 280 feet

T. 3-cyl. by Blair and Co. Ltd., Stockton-on-Tees

Cabo Roche was one of many Spanish vessels caught up in the country's brutal Civil War. She took refuge at Gibraltar in 1936, but on 25th June 1937 surrendered to the Nationalist gunboat *Lauria* in the Straits of Gibraltar, and ran for the Nationalists as *Gadofia* from 1937 to 1939. She then reverted to her original owners, Ybarra & Co., and as *Cabo Roche* survived until 1964 when she was broken up at Barcelona. She was photographed carrying a deck cargo of logs on 10th May 1944.

CABO SILLEIRO

Compania Euskalduna de Construcciones, Bilbao; 1915, 2,896gt, 306 feet

T. 3-cyl. by Central Marine Engine Works, West Hartlepool

Another Ybarra ship, but one with a rather complex history. She was built as *Mar Mediterraneo*, and passed in 1928 to Compania Trasmediterránea as *Rio Miño*, being sold to Ybarra and renamed *Cabo Silleiro* in 1935. In 1936 she was taken over by Gobierno de Euzkadi - the local government of the Basque region - to become *Anzora*. She too was captured by the Nationalists, in this case at Bilbao in June 1937, and was renamed *Roosile*. In 1939 it was again a case of restoration to Ybarra and her former name *Cabo Silleiro*, as seen in this photograph from 27th March 1944. Intimate details of her cargo can be seen, including barrels in the after hold, from which the hatch covers have been removed. *Cabo Silleiro* was broken up at Burriana late in 1964.

EA

S.P. Austin and Son, Sunderland; 1896, 1,269gt, 235 feet

T. 3-cyl. by John Dickinson and Sons Ltd., Sunderland

The long raised quarter deck identifies *Ea* as a British North Sea collier, although she is unusual in having three hatches ahead of her bridge rather than just two. She was ordered by J. and C. Harrison Ltd., London as *Harborne*, but before she was delivered her owners had merged with other collier companies to become William Cory and Sons Ltd. However, it was not until 1920 that a 'corporate' naming scheme saw her become *Corburn*, and this lasted only a year until she was sold to Spain as *Ea*. There were several changes of ownership during the next thirty years, and owners at the time she was photographed were Compañia Anonima Navieros del Norte, San Sebastian. Like most Spanish ships, her life was protracted, and after a change of name to *Somió* in 1952 she steamed on until broken up at Santander in 1968.

CAPITAN SEGARRA

Compañia Euskalduna de Construcciones, Bilbao; 1918, 2,252gt, 265 feet

T. 3-cyl. by Central Marine Engine Works, West Hartlepool

Passenger ships of Compañia Trasmediterránea featured prominently in the previous 'Spying on Spain' feature (Record 27) and this is one of their cargo ships approaching port on 1st October 1944. *Capitan Segarra* was built for the company's various cross-Mediterranean services and stayed on them until broken up at Bilbao in 1970.

ITA

A.G. 'Neptun', Rostock; 1902, 2,562gt, 291 feet

T. 3-cyl. by A.G. 'Neptun', Rostock

This German-built ship came into Spanish hands during the First World War. The Lubeck-owned *Eriphia* found herself in Bilbao in August 1914, and remained there throughout hostilities. The Spanish Government acquired her in 1918 and renamed her, somewhat unimaginatively, *España No. 1*. She was sold to commercial owners in 1924 as *Sardiñero*, and became *Ita* in 1934 for Compañia Federico G. Fierro, San Esteban de Pravia.

Adventures in the Spanish Civil War included being scuttled by the Republicans to block the entrance to the port of Huelva in August 1936. She was refloated once the port was in Nationalist hands, repaired, and returned to her owners. When *Ita* was broken up at Malaga in 1977 she had reached the venerable age of 75. This aerial photograph is dated 28th August 1944.

EL MONTECILLO

Dunlop, Bremner and Co. Ltd., Port Glasgow; 1920, 3,083gt, 329 feet

T. 3-cyl. by Dunlop, Bremner and Co. Ltd., Port Glasgow

Like *El Condado* this Clyde-built ship remained part of the Alejandro Navajas fleet throughout her life, being demolished in Bilbao during 1972. She is carrying a heavy cargo of logs.

CANDINA

Tyne Iron Shipbuilding Co., Newcastle-upon-Tyne; 1897, 2,587gt, 313 feet

T. 3-cyl. by North Eastern Marine Engineering Co. Ltd., Newcastle-upon-Tyne

Photographed on 24th June 1944, *Candina* is a fine example of a British-built tramp, probably largely unchanged since completed 47 years earlier as *Gloxinia* for Stag Line Ltd. *Gloxinia* was sold to a company managed by the Walford family in 1916, becoming *Petingaudet*. When the Walford group began to dispose of its expensively-acquired wartime ships, she went to Spain in 1921 as *Francisca Uravain*. The name *Candina* was bestowed on her in 1928, being the family name of one of her co-owners, and she retained this through several changes of ownership for a remarkable 38 years until she was broken up at Santander in 1966. The funnel markings are probably those of Compañia Naviera Española S.A. of Madrid. Owners at the time of the photograph were Compañia Naviera Bidasoa, a company which had owned her previously and was still associated with her owners.

EL CONDADO

William Hamilton and Co. Ltd., Port Glasgow; 1920, 3,492gt, 330 feet

T. 3-cyl. by Dunlop, Bremner and Co. Ltd., Port Glasgow

Most ships in this feature display their nationality prominently, but on 24th June 1944 *El Condado* has the names and flags of both Spain and Switzerland. Like neutral Ireland, Switzerland was desperate to obtain ships to carry essential imports, and where it could not buy ships it had no option but to charter them.

Remarkably, *El Condado* remained in the ownership or management of Alejandro Navajas, Bilbao throughout her 56-year career, which ended at a Spanish shipbreaking yard in 1976.

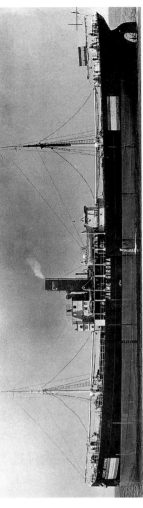

JACINTO VERDAGEUR
William Hamilton and Co. Ltd., Port Glasgow; 1900, 1,641gt, 245 feet
T. 3-cyl. David Rowan and Co., Glasgow

Photographed in October 1943, this elegant, clipper-bowed steamer was built as *Cid* for Compañía Trasmediterránea Marítima, Barcelona, a company which became one of the components of Compañía Trasmediterránea in 1917 when she was renamed *Jacinto Verdaguer*. She retained this name for almost forty years: it survived a transfer of ownership to Isleña Marítima S.A. in 1952, and remained until she was broken up in 1956. It would be interesting to know whether she still had the clipper bow.

PUNTA ALMINA
Carmichael, Maclean and Co., Greenock; 1897, 1,080gt, 226 feet
T. 3-cyl. Hutson and Co., Glasgow

To *Punta Almina* goes the dubious honour of most previous names, and having become a constructive total loss in original ownership. Built for J. Lauritzen of Esbjerg as *Nautik*, Spanish ownership began after she stranded off Ibiza Roads on 22nd February 1914, having broken an anchor chain while waiting to load. Abandoned to the underwriters as a constructive total loss, she lay there for some time, but the outbreak of war stimulated efforts to salve her, and she was refloated and repaired as *Enriqueta de Mallol* by 1915. Then began her series of renamings: *Santiago Mumbrú* in 1917; *Yturri-Ederra* in 1918, a Basque name which was also rendered *Iturri-Ederra*; *Castellón* in 1927, *Mari Eli* in 1930; *Castellón* again and *Castillo Cuéllar* as a Nationalist transport in 1938; briefly *Mari Eli* on return to her owners in 1941, and finally *Punta Almina* later in 1941. After this breathless renaming, *Punta Almina* she was to remain until broken up at her home port of Bilbao in August 1960, although she did manage a few changes of owner. A. Echevarria of Bilbao is recorded as her owner when photographed. Note the Royal Navy boat crew alongside the stationary steamer.

JAIME GERONA
Ropner and Son, Stockton-on-Tees; 1891, 2,434, 290 feet
T. 3-cyl. by Blair and Co. Ltd., Stockton-on-Tees

This Tees-built tramp steamer appears to be flush-decked, but closer examination suggests all but the second hatch is in a well. *Jaime Gerona* had a long and interesting life, including at least one major casualty. She was built as *Elwick* for Thomas Appleby and Co. of West Hartlepool, an owner once associated with her builders. After ownership by other obscure north east coast owners, she was sold to Spain in 1913 as *Trece*, becoming *Jaime Gerona* in 1916. Owned in Bilbao, she remained under Republican control during the Civil War, but struck a rock in Santander Bay on 25th March 1937 whilst on a voyage from Gijon to Bilbao with coal. The Civil War meant she was left beached in Santander Bay until refloated in May 1940, repaired and returned to service. Soon after this photograph was taken in June 1943 she was renamed *R. Ridaura* by Compañía Valenciana de Cementos Portland S.A., Valencia. She was broken up at Alicante in 1967.

JOSE TARTIERE
McDougall Duluth Shipbuilding Co., Duluth, Minnesota; 1920, 2,289gt, 251 feet
T. 3-cyl. by McDougall Duluth Shipbuilding Co., Duluth, Minnesota

Photographed on 7th June 1944, this neat little Great Lakes-built steamer was completed as *Josefa* for owners in Vigo. In 1928 she took the name *José Tartiere* for Compañía de Naviera Vasco-Asturiana. During 1936 and 1937 some vessels belonging to ports controlled by the Republicans were taken into a form of collective ownership, *José Tartiere* becoming *Genarin*. In 1937 she was restored to her owner and former name which she kept until broken up at Bilbao in March 1965.

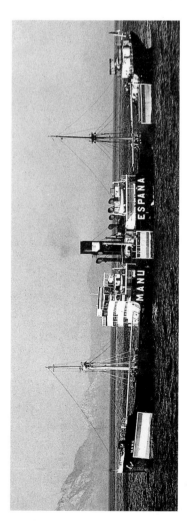

MANU

Tidewater Shipbuilders Ltd., Three Rivers, Port Quebec; 1921, 3,314gt, 331 feet
T. 3-cyl. by Tidewater Shipbuilders Ltd., Three Rivers, Port Quebec

Manu came from the little-known Canadian First World War shipbuilding programme: she was completed as *Canadian Fisher* much too late for hostilities. The Canadian Government tried rather unsuccessfully to manage these ships, and *Canadian Fisher* was sold to Spain in 1928, her new owner Compañia Naviera Amaya of Bilbao renaming her *Manu*.

On 30th October 1936 she was captured by the Nationalist battleship *España* whilst en route from the UK to Saltacaballo. The Nationalists placed her under the nominal ownership of Robert M. Sloman junior of Hamburg as *Marion*, presumably thinking that she would be less likely to be recaptured under a 'neutral' flag although, in reality, Nazi Germany was anything but neutral. With the Civil War going the Nationalists' way, she was restored to her owner and previous name in 1938. She is in this ownership in the photograph, taken 8th June 1944. The relatively modern-looking *Manu* lasted until 1976, when she was broken up at Cartagena.

MAR CARIBE

Sociedad Española de Construcciones Naval, Bilbao; 1920, 4,716gt, 358 feet
T. 3-cyl. J.G. Kincaid and Co. Ltd. Greenock

Another ship to have had just one name throughout her career, *Mar Caribe* was owned by Compañia Maritima del Nervion (Urquijo y Aldecoa, managers) of Bilbao, apart from a short spell in Republican hands during the Civil War, until broken up at her home port in 1964. The photograph was taken on 28th July 1944, and shows the very unusual lattice bipod masts, plus lattice derricks. She also has what appear to be emergency liferafts rigged alongside both masts.

LUIS ADARA

Richardson, Duck and Co., Stockton-on-Tees; 1888, 2,285gt, 273 feet
T. 3-cyl. by Blair and Co. Ltd. Stockton-on-Tees

Luis Adara is the oldest ship in this feature, although others survived longer. She was built on the Tees as *Somerhill* for London owners, and sold to Spain in 1913 when she was already a veteran of 25 years. She first became *Wenceslao*, taking the name *Luis Adara* in 1923 when bought by F. Gumersindo Junquera of Gijon, in whose ownership she was photographed on 9th July 1944. She was not to last much longer: on 2nd February 1946 she was wrecked near Pasajes whilst inward bound from Santander with a cargo of phosphate.

MAR NEGRO

Compañia Euskalduna, Bilbao; 1930; 6,632gt, 404 feet
Oil engines 4SCSA 16-cyl. by Akt. Burmeister & Wain, Copenhagen driving twin screws

Photographed on 22nd July 1944, *Mar Negro* was one of the relatively few modern motorships in the Spanish fleet. This may have been why she was commissioned by the Nationalists as an auxiliary cruiser in May 1938, after her master had put into the Italian port of Cagliari in September 1937 and surrendered her.

In 1939 *Mar Negro* was returned to the ownership of Compañia Maritima del Nervion (Urquijo y Aldecoa, managers), as seen here. Subsequent names were *Rio Pisuena* under the Spanish flag from 1968 and *Rio Frio* for Mexican owners from 1971. She was broken up at Kaohsiung in 1973.

INDEX TO RECORD 25 TO 28

Record 25: pp.1-64; Record 26: 65-128; Record 27: 129-192; Record 28: 193-264

Index of articles

Index of ships